Pandita Ramabai Sarasvati

The High-Caste Hindu Woman

Pandita Ramabai Sarasvati

The High-Caste Hindu Woman

ISBN/EAN: 9783744718196

Printed in Europe, USA, Canada, Australia, Japan

Cover: Foto ©ninafisch / pixelio.de

More available books at **www.hansebooks.com**

THE
HIGH-CASTE HINDU WOMAN.

BY

PUNDITA RAMABAI SARASVATI.

WITH INTRODUCTION BY

RACHEL L. BODLEY, A.M., M.D.,

DEAN OF WOMAN'S MEDICAL COLLEGE OF PENNSYLVANIA.

PHILADELPHIA:
1887.

Entered according to Act of Congress, in the year 1887, by
RAMABAI DONGRE MEDHAVI,
in the Office of the Librarian of Congress. All rights reserved.

Press of The Jas. B. Rodgers Printing Co.

TO THE

MEMORY OF MY BELOVED MOTHER,

LAKSHMĪBAI ˙DONGRE,

WHOSE SWEET INFLUENCE AND ABLE INSTRUCTION

HAVE BEEN

THE LIGHT AND GUIDE OF MY LIFE,

THIS LITTLE VOLUME

IS MOST REVERENTLY DEDICATED.

In Memoriam.

ANANDIBAI JOSHEE, M. D.

DAUGHTER OF GANPATRAO AMRITASWAR
AND
GUNGABAI JOSHEE.

Born in Poona, Bombay Presidency, India, March 31st, 1865. (Child-name, Yamuna Joshee.)

Married Gopalrao Vinayak Joshee, March 31st, 1874. (Wife-name, Anandibai Joshee.)

Sailed from Calcutta, India, for America, April 7th, 1883, being the first high-caste Brahman woman to come to the United States. Landed in New York, June 4th, 1883.

Graduated in medicine, from the Woman's Medical College of Pennsylvania, March 11th, 1886, being the first Hindu woman to receive the Degree of Doctor of Medicine in any country.

Appointed, June 1st, 1886, to the position of Physician-in-Charge of the Female Ward of the Albert Edward Hospital, in the City of Kolhapur, India.

Sailed from New York, to assume her duties in Kolhapur, October 9th, 1886.

Died in Poona, India, February 26th, 1887.

INTRODUCTION.

THE silence of a thousand years has been broken, and the reader of this unpretending little volume catches the first utterances of the unfamiliar voice. Throbbing with woe, they are revealed in the following pages to intelligent, educated, happy American women.

God grant that these women, whom He has blessed above all women upon the earth, may not flippantly turn away, as they are wont to do from some overpious tale, and without reading, condemn! To begin this story of *The High-caste Hindu Woman*, and not to read it through attentively to the last word of the agonized appeal, is to invoke upon oneself the divine displeasure meted out to those who disregard the cry of "him that had none to help him." These lines are written with deep emotion; the blinding tears which fall upon the page are the saddest tears my eyes have ever wept.

From childhood I had been familiar with the statements concerning the condition of the native women of India. My sympathies had always been with them, and my annual offering to the treasury of missionary societies which worked among them, had never been omitted; but in September, 1883, there came to my door a little lady in a blue cotton *saree*, accompanied by her faithful friend, Mrs. B. F. Carpenter, of Roselle, New Jersey, and since that hour, when, speechless for very wonder, I bestowed a kiss of welcome upon the stranger's cheek in lieu of words, I have loved the women of India. The little lady was Mrs. Anandibai Joshee. Less than three months ago, the wealthy and conservative city of Poona, India, which gave her birth, was stirred as never before to honor a woman, and amid the pomp of Brahmanical funeral rites performed by orthodox Hindu priests, her funeral pile was lighted from the sacred fire, in the presence of a great throng of sorrowing Hindus. She sealed with her early death the superhuman effort to elevate her countrywomen and to minister in her own person to their physical needs.

To witness Dr. Joshee's graduation in medicine, there came to Philadelphia from England her kinswoman, Pundita Ramabai Sarasvati. The two ladies never met until they greeted each other under my roof, March 6th, 1886; but, as kindred spirits, they had corresponded for several years. Strangely enough, each left India without the knowledge of the other, and within the same month, Mrs. Joshee sailing from Calcutta and the Pundita from Bombay. The day that Mrs. Joshee left Liverpool for New York, Ramabai and her little daughter landed in England. The reception of the two ladies in the summer of 1883, one in England and the other in the United States, was most cordial; and, comforted and blessed as neither had dared to anticipate before leaving India, each settled down to work with industry and with

Introduction. iii

a degree of intelligence which was a revelation to on-lookers.

My own personal experience relates to her who fell to our lot in the college in Philadelphia. She tried faithfully, this little woman of eighteen, to prosecute her studies, and at the same time to keep caste-rules and cook her own food; but the anthracite coal-stove in her room was a constant vexation, and likewise a source of danger; and the solitude of the individual house-keeping was overwhelming. In her father's house, the congregate system, referred to in this book, prevailed; and, being a man of means, the family was always large. Later, when under her husband's care, he had been in the postal service, and the dwelling apartments were in the same building with the post-office; hence she had never known complete solitude. After a trial of two weeks, her health declined to such an alarming extent that I invited her to pay a short visit in my home, and she never left it again to dwell elsewhere in Philadelphia during her student residence. In the performance of college duties, going in and out, and up and down, always in her measured, quiet, dignified, patient way, she has filled every room, as well as the stairways and halls, with memories which now hallow the home, and must continue so to do throughout the years to come.

In the spring of 1884, Mrs. Joshee accepted an invitation to address an audience of ladies convened for a missionary anniversary, and she chose as her subject "Child Marriage," and surprised her great audience by defending the national custom. If there are any who still cherish the feelings of disappointment and regret engendered that April afternoon, let them turn to Ramabai's chapter on Married Life in this book, and learn how absolutely impossible it was for a high-caste Hindu wife to speak otherwise. Let them also discover, in the herculean attempt of that occasion, a clue to the influences which at length overpowered and slew this gentle, grave woman.

"I will go (to America) as a Hindu, and come back and live among my people as a Hindu." Brave, patriotic words! a resolve which was carried out to the death. Ramabai's chapter on Married Life, the married life of a Hindu woman in the year 1887, no less than in past centuries, reveals to the Western reader what it was for this refined, intellectual woman, whose faculties developed rapidly under Western opportunities, and whose scientific acquirements placed her high in rank among her peers in the college class, to accept again the position awarded her by the Code of Manu (Manu ix. 22; see page 40). That she did accept it, that "until death she was patient of hardships, self-controlled, . . . and strove to fulfill that most excellent duty which is prescribed for wives," is undoubted. She battled hand to hand with every circumstance, resolved, as a Hindu, to live and work for the uplifting of her sisters, but all in vain!

After years of exile, she found herself once more in the familiar places of her childhood, surrounded by her mother and maternal grandmother and sisters. She had returned to them too late to admit of the restoration of her appetite by the nourishing food their skillful hands knew how to prepare; but in love they watched beside her, and it was the dear mother's privilege to support the daughter in her arms when at midnight the end came quickly. This occurred February 26th, 1887, in the city of Poona, in the house in which she was born. Previous to the cremation of the body, which took place the morning following her death, her husband had a photograph taken of "matter before it was transformed into vapor and ashes." The pathos of that lifeless form is indescribable. The last of several pictures, taken during the brief public career of the little reformer, it is the most eloquent of them all. The mute lips, and the face, wan and wasted and prematurely aged in the fierce battle with sorrow and pain, alike convey to her American friends this message, not to be forgotten: "I have done all that I could do." Ah! who will thus early dare to say that she has not accomplished more by her death than she might have accomplished by a long life? Herself and husband returned from a foreign land, where they had dwelt with a strange people, ought, by Hindu custom, to have been treated as outcasts, and their shadows shunned. Instead, when it was known that the distinguished young Hindu doctor had reached her early home, old and young, orthodox and non-orthodox, came to pay friendly visits and to extend a cordial welcome.

Even the reformers were astounded when they beheld the manner in which the travelers were treated by the most orthodox families. The papers from day to day chronicled the state of the invalid's health, and when at length she passed away, several of the journals of Poona printed in the vernacular, contained under symbols of mourning, eulogistic notices of her character and work. Ramabai has translated two of these for me, and from them I make extracts:

"Dr. Anandibai Joshee has left us to abide in the next world; but the example she has set will not be fruitless. It is indeed wonderful that a Brahman lady has proved to the world that the great qualities—perseverance, unselfishness, undaunted courage and an eager desire to serve one's country—do exist in the so-called weaker sex. We ought as a people to do something that will remind us of her and bear witness forever to her wondrous virtues ; in our opinion, this debt of gratitude to Anandibai cannot be better discharged than by providing a lady, who will be willing to study medicine, with all the pecuniary aid necessary. Thus may the memory of the late distinguished lady be perpetuated."—*Kesari, February 27, 1887.*

"One of the great and grievous losses which our unfortunate Hindustan incessantly sustains was witnessed by Poona, we grieve to say, on Saturday last, when Dr. Anandibai Joshee was summoned from this world late in the midnight. She has been residing in Poona for the last two months ; she came hither in the hope that her native city, which has many renowned physicians residing in it, might prove for her a healthy place, and that the pleasant weather and home influences would all contribute towards improving her health. The hopeful expectations of her countrywomen, who had looked forward to the day when they would be benefited by Dr. Joshee's remarkable ability and well-earned knowledge, are now wholly dissipated."

"Although Anandibai was so young, her perseverance, undaunted courage and devotion to her husband were unparalleled. We think it will be long before we shall again see a woman like her in this country. We do not hesitate to say that Dr. Joshee is worthy of a high place on the roll of historic women who have striven to serve and to elevate their native land. . . . The education that she had received had greatly heightened her nature and ennobled her mind. Although she suffered more than words can express from her mortal disease, phthisis, not a word either of complaint or impatience escaped her lips at any time. After months of dreadful suffering she was reduced to skin and bone, and every one that looked at her could not but be greatly pained ; yet, wonderful to relate, Anandibai thought it her present duty to suffer silently and cheerfully. . . . After the picture was taken, her relatives bathed the body and decked it with bright garments and ornaments, according to Hindu custom. There was no time to spread the sad news throughout the city, but as many as heard it

Introduction. vii

accompanied her remains to the cremation ground, thus showing the respectful affection they felt for her. Some people had feared that the priests might raise objections to cremating her body in the sacred fire, according to the Hindu rites; but these fears proved groundless. Not only on the occasion of her cremation, but earlier during her lifetime, when her husband offered sacrifices to the gods and the guardian planets to avert their anger and her death, the priests showed no sign of any prejudice against them; they gladly officiated in the religious sacrifices, thus affording a remarkable proof of their advanced views. After the body was placed upon the funeral pile Mr. V. M. Ranade made an oration in Dr. Joshee's honor, and the cremation was then completed without hindrance."—*Dnyana Chakshu, March 2nd,* 1887.

The general public interest in the person and work of Dr. Joshee is a sufficient reason for presenting in this introductory chapter the above details, which have not elsewhere been given to her American friends. Pundita Ramabai, her beloved and trusted kinswoman, still lives to perform, not her identical work, but to prosecute the general disenthrallment of Hindu women, concerning the ultimate accomplishment of which Dr. Joshee cherished invincible faith. Greatly bereaved, her fond hopes of a congenial supporter and an efficient helper in India suddenly dashed to the ground, Ramabai toils on with a heroic singleness of purpose. It is in the prosecution of this one supreme object of helping her countrywomen to a better and higher life that this little book has been written. In her contact with American philanthropists and educators, during the year of her sojourn in the United States, Ramabai has found popular ideas concerning the women of India erroneous, and it is to correct these, and also to reveal fully their needs, that the following chapters have been prepared.

She has written in the belief that if the depths of

the thralldom in which the dwellers in Indian zenanas are held by cruel superstition and social customs were only fathomed, the light and love in American homes, which have so comforted her burdened heart, might flow forth in an overwhelming tide to bless all Indian women. The task of preparing *The High-caste Hindu Woman* has not been for her a congenial one. She is not by nature an iconoclast. She loves her nation with a pure, strong love. But her love has reached the height where it is akin to the motive of the skillful surgeon: she dares to inflict pain because she regards pain as affording the only sure means of relief. She is satisfied, moreover, that India cannot arise and take her place among the nations of the earth until she, too, has mothers; until the Hindu zenana is transformed into the Hindu home, where the united family can have "pleasant times together" (see p. 48).

The experiment of bringing the existing condition of high-caste Hindu women to the test of codes of sacred law, it is believed, was never before attempted. The reader will bear in mind, as she cons the carefully selected texts from the Code of Manu which abound throughout the volume, that these are sentences too sacred for feminine lips to utter, and that few women in India have ever heard them, much less have beheld them with their own eyes. Even Ananta Shastri, liberal as he was in his views concerning the education of women, withheld the sacred texts from his wife and daughters. The Sanskrit literature accessible to them, consisted of poems not associated with sacred rites and ceremonies. Ramabai never saw a copy of the Code of Manu until after her scholastic attainments had been publicly recognized in Calcutta.

She has exercised great care in securing correctness

in her quotations, diligently comparing translations, where more than one were available, and in some cases making the translation herself from the original Sanskrit. The general statements throughout the book may be relied upon for their accuracy. Should the volume reach India, these statements will undoubtedly be assailed as untruthful and sacrilegious, and possibly there may be persons in the United States who will strive to create this impression; but Ramabai's desire to speak the truth is only equalled by her determination to let in the full blaze of day upon effete customs and perilous usages. She has withheld nothing essential that her wide experience throughout India has revealed to her. She does not print this information for the purpose of reputation or of gain, but because taught, as she believes, by the Divine Spirit, that the revelation will stir the hearts of those who read the story to deeds of rescue and relief.

There are readers who, upon the title-page of this book, will see the Pundita's name for the first time, and all such will naturally inquire, Who is ⁎ she? In view of the fact, that she seeks to assume grave responsibilities before the American public this question is legitimate, and therefore, at the risk of growing tedious, I will endeavor to make answer. It is a weird beginning of a life-sketch to ask the inquirer to turn to page 37 and read of an occurrence, in the early morning, on the banks of the sacred river Godavari. The fine-looking man who came to the river-side to bathe was the learned Ananta Shastri, and the little girl of nine, whom he carried away the day following as his child-bride, was Ramabai's mother. This Brahman pundit, who "well and tenderly cared for the little girl beyond all expectation," was a native of the Mangalore district in Western India.

In his boyhood, when about ten years of age, he had been married, and had brought his child-bride to his mother's house and committed the little girl to her keeping. He, however, was possessed with a desire for the acquisition of knowledge, and attracted by the fame of Ramachandra Shastri, a distinguished scholar, who dwelt in Poona, he early made his way thither, and sought his instruction. This eminent Brahman had been employed by the reigning Peshwa to visit his palace statedly, and give Sanskrit lessons to a favorite wife. The student Ananta was privileged to accompany his teacher, and, thus going in and out of the palace, he occasionally heard the lady reciting Sanskrit poems.

The boy was filled with wonder that a woman should be so learned, and as time wore on, astonishment gave place to admiration of her learning, and he resolved that he would teach his little wife just as the Shastri taught the fair Rani of the palace. His student-life ended at the age of twenty-three, and he hastened to his native village to incorporate education with his duties as a householder. But the bride had no desire to be instructed; his mother and all the elders of the family demurred, and the husband was compelled to desist. The married life went on, children were born to the young couple, and at length the wife died. The widower had not forgotten the Peshwa's palace in Poona and the Sanskrit poems, and he resolved to begin his next experiment early.

We learn from the printed page how he accepted the little bride of nine who was offered to him, and carried her to his distant home; there he delivered her to his mother, and immediately began to teach her Sanskrit. But the elders of the household objected as before; the little wife was too young to have a voice in the matter, and the husband resolved that the experiment of the girl's education should be faithfully carried out. He therefore left the valley and civilization below him, and journeyed upward with his young wife to the forest of Gungamul, on a remote plateau of the Western Ghauts, and literally in the jungle, took up his abode. Ramabai relates as a memory of her childhood her mother's recital of how the first night was spent in the sylvan solitude, without shelter of any kind. A great tiger came with the darkness, and from across a ravine, made the night hideous with its cries. The little bride wrapped herself up tight in her *pasodi* (cotton quilt) and lay upon the ground convulsed with terror, while the husband kept watch until daybreak, when the hungry beast disappeared. The wild animals of the jungle were all about them, and hourly terrified the lonely little girl; but the lessons went on without hindrance, and day by day the wife, Lakshmibai, grew in stature and in knowledge. A rude dwelling was constructed, and after a few years little children came to the home in the forest,—one son and two daughters. The father devoted himself to the education of the son and elder daughter, and also to that of young men who, as students, sought out the now famous Brahman priest, whose dwelling-place in the mountains, at the source of one of the rivers, was regarded as sacred, and hence a place of pilgrimage for the pious. When Ramabai, the youngest child, was born, in April, 1858, the father was quite too much occupied to instruct her, and, moreover, he was growing old. Upon her mother, therefore, devolved the instruction in Sanskrit.

The resident students and the visiting pilgrims and the aged father and mother-in-law, now members of the family, as well as the children of the household, entailed many cares upon the educated Hindu mother, and the only time that could be found for the little daughter's lessons was in the morning twilight, before the toilsome day had dawned. Ramabai recalls with emotion that early instruction while held in her dear mother's arms. The little maiden, heavy with sleep, was tenderly lifted from her bed upon the earth, and wakened with many endearments and sweet mother-words; and then, while the birds about them in the forest chirped their morning songs, the lessons were repeated, no other book than the mother's lips being used. It is these lessons of the early morning, statedly renewed with each recurrent day, that constitute the fountain-head of the "sweet influences and able instruction" which, in the dedicatory page of this book, the author characterizes as "the light and guide of my life."

But this was a Hindu home, not an American home where such kindly care and wise parental love would have borne for the parents refreshing fruit in their old age. The father, under the iron rule of custom, had given his elder daughter in marriage when very young, and upon pages 62 and 63 we learn the nature of the sorrows which overtook the family; previous to this, however, the popularity of the Shastri as a teacher, and his sacred locality in the wilderness, had involved him in debt; for guests must be fed and duties enjoined by religion performed, at whatever pecuniary loss. The half of his landed property in his native village, which was to be the portion of the son by the second wife, was, with the son's consent, sold to discharge the debts, and then the family, homeless, set out upon pilgrimages. It is difficult for the Western reader, with whom the word home is inseparable from family existence, to realize that this Hindu family were thus employed seven years, Ramabai being nine years of age when they set out.

But all the while as this Marathi priest and his wife

and children wandered from one sacred locality to the next, having no certain dwelling-place, the early morning lessons were continued, and Ramabai, developing rare talent, became, under the instructions of father and mother, "a prodigy of erudition." Engrossed in her studies, she was allowed to remain single until the age of sixteen, when, within a month and a half of each other, her parents died.

"From my earliest years," Ramabai states, "I always had a love of books. Though I was not formally taught Marathi, yet hearing my father and mother speak it and being in the habit of reading newspapers and books in that language, I acquired a correct knowledge of it. In this manner I acquired also the knowledge of Kanarese, Hindustani and Bengali while traveling about. My father and mother did not do with me as others were in the habit of doing with their daughters, *i. e.*, throw me into the well of ignorance by giving me in marriage in my infancy. In this my parents were both of one mind." When death invaded the pilgrim household, the father, bowed with age and now totally blind for several years, was taken first; in six weeks the mother followed. The poverty of the family was extreme; consequently, Brahmans could not be secured to bear the remains to the burning-ghat, which was three miles distant from the scene of the mother's death. At length two Brahmans were found who took pity upon them, and with the assistance of these men, the devoted son and daughter themselves carried the precious burden to the distant place of cremation, Ramabai's low stature compelling the bearing of her share of the burden upon her head. Why do I recount this passage of nameless woe? Why? Because we American women, in our own homes, have never before looked into the face of one upon whom a ministry of sorrow so overwhelming as this has been laid, and we need, in our prosperity, to realize that God hath made of one blood all nations of men. The lovely woman who writes this book in the city of Philadelphia and the beloved mother to whom she dedicates it were in the forest of Gungamul and in the later, dusty paths of pilgrimage alike destitute of the true knowledge of God; but, in their great spiritual darkness, they ministered to and mutually loved and cherished each other with that maternal and filial affection which is the same the world over.

After the death of the parents and the elder sister, Ramabai and her brother continued to travel. They visited many countries on the great continent of India, the Punjab, Rajputana, the Central Provinces, Assam, Bengal and Madras, and, as pilgrims, were often in want and distress. They spent their time in advocating female education, *i. e.*, that before marriage high-caste Hindu girls should be instructed in Sanskrit and in their vernacular, according to the ancient Shastras.

When, in their journeying, they at length reached Calcutta, the young Sanskrit scholar and lecturer created a sensation by her advanced views and her scholarship. She was summoned before the assembled pundits of the capital city; and as a result of their examination the distinguished title of Sarasvati was publicly conferred upon her by them. Soon after, her brother died. "His great thought during his brief illness," she writes, "was for me; what would become of me left alone in the world? When he spoke of his anxiety, I answered: 'There is no one but God to care for you and me.' 'Ah,' he answered, 'then if God cares for us, I am afraid of nothing.' And, indeed, in my loneliness, it seemed as if God was near me; I felt His presence." "After six months I mar-

Introduction.

ried a Bengali gentleman, Bipin Bihari Medhavi, M.A., B.L., a Vakil and a graduate of the Calcutta University. But we neither of us believed either in Hinduism or Christianity, and so we were married with the civil marriage rite. . . . After nineteen months of happy married life, my dear husband died of cholera. This great grief drew me nearer to God. I felt that He was teaching me, and that if I was to come to Him, He must Himself draw me." A few months before the husband's death a little daughter was born in the happy home—a daughter greatly desired by both father and mother before her birth, and hence, she found a beautiful name awaiting her,—Manorama (*Heart's Joy*).

The widow Ramabai now returned to her former occupation as a lecturer. It became her especial mission to advocate the cause of Hindu women, according to what she believed to be the true rendering of the ancient Shastras, in opposition to the degraded notions of modern times. Her earnestness and enthusiasm gained her many admirers, among whom was Dr. W. W. Hunter, prominently connected with the British educational interests of India. He thought her career and the good she was doing so well worthy of admiration that he made her the subject of a lecture delivered in Edinburgh.

"When I spoke," says Dr. Hunter, "of a high-caste Indian lady being thus employed, that great English audience rose as one man and applauded the efforts which the Pundita Ramabai was making on behalf of her countrywomen." Henceforth her name was well known in England, as well as in India, to all who were interested in the social amelioration of the people of Hindustan.

With a view to improve the degraded condition of her countrywomen, she formed in Poona a society of ladies, known as the *Arya Mahila Somaj*, whose object was the promotion of education among native women, and the discouragement of child-marriage. She then went from city to city throughout the Bombay Presidency, establishing branch societies and arousing the people by her eloquent appeals. When the English Education Commission visited Poona in September, 1882, for the purpose of inspecting the educational institutions of that city, the leading Brahman ladies, members of the newly-formed society and others, to the number of about three hundred, assembled with their children in the Town Hall, to welcome the Commission and to show them that, although the municipality had not encouraged girls' schools, a genuine movement was being inaugurated by the best families of the Marathi country. Pundita Ramabai was the orator of the occasion.

Dr. Hunter, as President of the Education Commission, made Ramabai the prominent figure among the many noteworthy persons who were examined before him during that visit. He regarded her evidence as of so much importance that he caused it to be translated from the Marathi and separately printed. A copy of this India print is before me as I write. There are three questions, viz. :—

Question 1.—State what opportunities you have had of forming an opinion on the subject of Education in India, and in what province your experience has been gained?

Here follows, in reply, a brief, but remarkably clear, narrative of her parentage, her father's views, those of her brother, also a statement in regard to her husband, and the vicissitudes of her life; all of which, she stated, had afforded her many opportunities of forming an opinion on the subject of Female Education in different provinces of India. She closes thus :—

"'I am the child of a man who had to suffer a great deal on account

Introduction. xvii

of advocating Female Education, and who was compelled to discuss the subject, as well as to carry out his own views, amidst great opposition. . . . I consider it my duty, to the very end of my life, to maintain this cause, and to advocate the proper position of women in this land."

Question 2.—What is the best method of providing teachers for girls?

Answer 2.—It appears to me evident that the women who are to become teachers of others should have a special training for that work. Besides having a correct knowledge of their own language, they ought to acquire English. Whether those training to be female teachers are married or unmarried, or widows, they ought to be correct in their conduct and morals, and they ought also to be of respectable families. They ought to be provided with good scholarships. Teachers of girls also ought to have higher salaries than those of boys, as they should be of a superior character and position. The students should live in the college compound, so as to have their manners and habits improved, and there ought to be a large building with every appliance for the comfort of the teachers and students. They ought to have a native lady of good position over them. Mere learning is not enough; the conduct and morals of the students should be attended to.

Question 3.—What do you regard as the chief defects, other than any to which you have already referred, that experience has brought to light in the educational system as it has been hitherto administered? What suggestions have you to make for the remedy of such defects?

Answer 3.—There ought to be female inspectresses over female schools. These ought to be of the age of thirty or upwards, and of a very superior class, and highly educated, whether Native or European. Male inspectors are unsuitable for the following reasons:—(1) The women of this country are very timid. If a male inspector goes into a female school, all the women and girls are thrown into confusion, and are unable to speak. The inspector seeing this state of things will write a bad report of the school and teachers, and so in all probability Government will appoint a male teacher for that school, and so the school will not have the advantage of a female teacher. As the education of girls is different from that of boys, female schools ought to be in the hands of female teachers. (2) The second reason is this. In ninety-nine cases out of a hundred, the educated men of this country are opposed to Female Education and the proper position of woman. If they observe the slightest fault, they magnify the grain of mustard-seed into a mountain, and try to ruin the character of a woman; often the poor woman, not being very courageous, and well informed, her character is completely broken. Men being more able to reach the authorities are believed, while women go to the wall. Both should be alike to a parental Government, whose children, male and female, should be treated with equal justice. It is evident that women, being one-half of the people of this country, are oppressed and cruelly treated by the other half. To put a stop to this anomaly is worthy of a good Government. Another suggestion I would make is with regard to lady-doctors. Though in Hindustan there are numbers of gentleman-doctors, there are no ladies of that profession. The women of this country are much more reserved than in other countries, and most of them would rather die than speak of their ailments to a man. The want of lady-doctors is, therefore, the cause of hundreds of thousands of women dying prematurely deaths. I would, therefore, earnestly entreat of our Government to make provision for the study of medicine by women, and thus save the lives of those multitudes. The want of lady-doctors is one very much felt and is a great defect in the Education of the women of this country.

The answers to these questions are introduced in full, as bearing valuable and ample testimony to the character, and the position before the public, of Ramabai in her own country. Upon the authority of the *Times of India*, it may be stated that her plea for women-physicians before the Commission, in September, 1882, (See Answer 3), is believed to have attracted the attention of her gracious Majesty, the Queen-Empress, and to have been indirectly the origin of the movement in Hindustan which, in its latest developments, has reached the noble proportions of *The National Association for Supplying Female Medical Aid to the Women of India*, popularly known as the "Countess of Dufferin Movement," from its distinguished president, the wife of the Viceroy of India.

Ramabai now realized that she herself needed personal training to enable her to prosecute with success her work among the women of India in behalf of education. Then, too, as she had in her experience become conscious of God's guidance, her spirit was possessed of that unrest which is the solemn movement of the soul Godward, seeking "the Lord if haply she (they) might feel after Him and find Him." "I felt a restless desire to go to England," she writes. "I could not have done this unless I had felt that my faith in God had become strong: it is such a great step for a Hindu woman to cross the sea; one cuts oneself always off from one's people. But the voice came to me as to Abraham. . . . It seems to me now very strange how I could have started as I did with my friend and little child throwing myself on God's protection. I went forth as Abraham, not knowing whither I went. When I reached England, the Sisters in St. Mary's Home at Wantage kindly received me. There I gradually learned to feel the truth of Christianity, and to see that it is a philosophy, teaching truths higher than I had ever known in all our systems; to see that it gives not only precepts, but a perfect example; that it does not give us precepts and an example only, but assures us of divine grace, by which we can follow that example." True to her honest nature, she acted promptly upon her convictions and embraced Christianity, and she and her little daughter were baptized in the Church of England, September 29th, 1883. Henceforth she devoted herself to educational work. The first year was spent at Wantage in the study of the English language, which hitherto had been unknown to her. Acquiring this, she entered, September, 1884, the Ladies' College at Cheltenham, where a position was assigned her as Professor of Sanskrit. Her unoccupied time was spent as a student of the college, in the study of mathematics, natural science, and English literature. Her opportunities at Cheltenham College were of the highest order, and the influence of the noble Christian women with whom she was associated, both there and at Wantage, was most refined and salutary in its character. She made rapid progress in her studies, and a possible Government educational appointment in India loomed up in the near future, when an invitation reached her to witness Mrs. Joshee's graduation in medicine in Philadelphia, March 11th, 1886.

That "holy land called America" had long held attractions for her, and these were now heightened by the presence and work of her beloved kinswoman. After some weeks of painful indecision, she decided to accept the invitation, her sole reason for allowing her studies to be interrupted thus inopportunely being her thorough conviction that it was her duty in the interests of her countrywomen to visit America at that time. In February, 1886, she again embarked upon an unknown sea, accompanied by her young daughter, then nearly five years of age. Her residence in America and her public service here have been widely chronicled in the daily and weekly journals, and are not therefore a matter of private record. In the beginning she expected to return to England after a brief vacation, and there resume her studies; but, as the genius of American institutions was revealed through personal inspection, her interest grew, and she decided to prolong her stay. In midsummer she wrote: "I am deeply impressed by and am interested in the work of Western women, who seem to have one common aim, namely, the good of their fellow-beings. It is my dream some day to tell my countrywomen in their own languages this wonderful story, in the hope that the recital may awaken in their hearts a desire to do likewise." As her contact with a public educational system which included girls as well as boys was prolonged, her old desire to benefit her countrywomen by founding schools which combined the training of the hand with that of the head revived, and forsaking plans which regarded only the higher education of the few women in government high-schools or colleges in India, she concentrated her thoughts upon native schools founded by and for native women. Early in her residence in Philadelphia she met Miss Anna Hallowell, prominently identified with the Sub-Primary School Society (free kindergartens) of the city. This distinguished lady kindly accompanied her to several of the kindergartens, and explained methods to her with care, and also the principles upon which the system was based. Ramabai's enthusiasm was aroused as she saw in Froebel's teaching wondrous possibilities for her little widows. Purchasing without delay the most approved text-books and the "gifts," she set herself to work to translate into Indian thought the games and tokens of the system, in order that she might

Introduction. xxi

adapt it to Hindu needs. In September, 1886, she promptly enrolled herself as a student in a kindergarten training-school, and, as her public duties have permitted, she has faithfully pursued the course of study throughout the scholastic year just ending. American school-books were a revelation to her in the beauty of their illustrations and of their letter-press and the quality of the paper upon which they are printed. In July, 1886, she set herself to work upon a series of Marathi school-books for girls, modeled after the American idea, beginning with a primer and continuing regularly up to a reader of the sixth grade. She was enthusiastic as to results, designing to illustrate with American wood-cuts, although the printing would necessarily be delayed until Bombay is reached, on account of the Marathi type required. The primer was soon finished, and much of the material for the reading books prepared, when a prudent investigation was instituted as to the cost of illustrations, and the stern fact revealed that the charming pictures were far too expensive to be dreamed of for her books.

Thus the case stands June 1st, 1887. Pundita Ramabai, the high-caste Brahman woman, the courageous daughter of the forest, educated, refined, rejoicing in the liberty of the Gospel, and yet by preference retaining a Hindu's care as regards a vegetable diet, and the peculiarities of the dress of Hindu widowhood, solemnly consecrated to the work of developing self-help among the women of India, has her school-books nearly ready for the printer, her plans for the organization of a school, such as she describes on page 114, well developed, and two teachers (American ladies, one a graduated kindergartner) secured. Tickets for herself and teachers might be taken for India at once, and as a result of the strong reaction which the untimely death of Dr. Joshee has set up, Ramabai, outcast though she is among her own people, might inaugurate, under favorable auspices, her work among the child-widows.

But the money is wanting. In 1793, when William Carey, the first English missionary to Asia, was about to set sail for India, he said to those about him, "I will go down into the deep mine, but remember that you must hold the ropes." As I close this chapter, the longing fills my soul that among the favored women of this Christian land there might be found a sufficient number to hold the ropes for Ramabai, making it possible for her to go out quickly to her God-inspired work. It must not be a fitful benefaction of a few hundred or even of a few thousand dollars, but *a steady holding on to the ropes*, for a period of not less than ten years. They must not be let go while she in the throes of a death-struggle with superstition and caste prejudice, and feminine unwillingness to rise, is fastened to the India end.

A decade of years ago, no sane woman would have presumed to appeal to the women and young girls of this land to engage in a project such as this of Ramabai, as I now do. But how rapidly we are moving on in these last days! We read in prophecy that "the earth shall be made to bring forth in one day," and "a nation shall be born at once;" and another sure word is written, "the people shall be willing in the day of His power." When in that great Hindu nation about to come to the birth, the women are moved to arise in their degradation, and themselves utter the feeble cry, "Help or we perish!" it cannot be otherwise than that a corresponding multitude of women must be found elsewhere, willing, in the day of God's power, to send the help.

There have long been in every community, women who are not in accord with the so-called missionary

Introduction. xxiii

societies, and who never contribute to the enlightenment or to the material aid of Oriental women. Ramabai's boarding-school for child-widows, primarily an educational scheme, may be safely taken up by such, and while they organize, and after the manner of the women's boards of the churches, through a great network of auxiliary societies, prosecute with growing interest and zeal their child-widow school work, missionary work so-called, may be continued by the societies of every denomination, each according to its own methods, the treasuries of all being alike full.

The Pundita bears witness, in public and in private, to the good accomplished in the East by missionary lady-teachers, and it is her earnest desire not to affect unfavorably in any manner, however remote, either the treasury or the work of church societies. She seeks to reach Hindu women as Hindus, to give them liberty and latitude as regards religious convictions; she would make no condition as to reading the Bible or studying Christianity; but she designs to put within their reach in reading-books and on the shelves of the school library, side by side, *the Bible* and *the Sacred books of the East*, and for the rest, earnestly pray that God will guide them to His saving truth.

It is roughly computed that Ramabai will need about fifteen thousand dollars to fully inaugurate the work of her first school and five thousand dollars annually afterwards during the ten years for which she asks help.

So easy is it to plan, so difficult to execute! Ramabai herself offers a reasonable means by which the collection of this sum may be commenced, in the presentation of this, her only American book to the public. It has been privately printed, in order that the entire profits may accrue to her; in the hope of a possible large sale, the pages have been copyrighted and electrotyped. If, therefore, every American woman who, at any time during the last twelvemonth, has taken Ramabai by the hand, every college student who has heard the Pundita speak in college halls, every reader of this book whose heart has been stirred to compassion by the perusal of its sorrowful pages, will at once purchase a copy of the book and induce a friend to do the same, each reader being responsible for the sale of one copy, the work is done, and the large fund needed to prepay three passages to India, to purchase the illustrative material for the school-rooms, to illustrate and print the school-books, and secure the needed school-property in India, is at once assured.

Ramabai has come into my library to bid me farewell, previous to her setting out on a journey of a few days. I asked her as she arose to depart, if she had a last message for the readers of her book. "Remind them," she replied, with animated countenance and rapid speech, as she clasped my hand "that it was 'out of Nazareth' that the blessed Redeemer of mankind came; that great reforms have again and again been wrought by instrumentalities that the world despised. Tell them to help me educate the high-caste child-widows; for I solemnly believe that this hated and despised class of women, educated and enlightened, are, by God's grace, to redeem India!"

R. L. B.

1400 NORTH 21st ST., PHILADELPHIA,
June 1st, 1887.

CONTENTS.

CHAPTER I.
PREFATORY REMARKS, ... 1

CHAPTER II.
CHILDHOOD, ... 12

CHAPTER III.
MARRIED LIFE, ... 29

CHAPTER IV.
WOMAN'S PLACE IN RELIGION AND SOCIETY, ... 50

CHAPTER V.
WIDOWHOOD, ... 69

CHAPTER VI.
HOW THE CONDITION OF WOMEN TELLS UPON SOCIETY, 94

CHAPTER VII.
THE APPEAL, ... 107

THE
HIGH-CASTE HINDU WOMAN.

PREFATORY REMARKS.

IN order to understand the life of a Hindu woman, it is necessary for the foreign reader to know something of the religion and the social customs of the Hindu nation. The population of Hindustan numbers two hundred and fifty millions, and is made up of Hindus, Mahometans, Eurasians, Europeans and Jews; more than three-fifths of this vast population are professors of the so-called Hindu religion in one or the other of its forms. Among these the religious customs and orders are essentially the same; the social customs differ slightly in various parts of the country, but they have an unmistakable similarity underlying them.

The religion of the Hindus is too vast a subject to be fully treated in a few paragraphs; it may be briefly stated, however, somewhat thus:—All Hindus recognize the Vedas and other apocryphal books as the canonical scriptures. They believe in one supreme spirit, Paramatma, which is pure, passionless, omnipresent, holy and formless in its essence, but when it is influenced by Maya, or illusion, it assumes form, becomes male and female, creates every thing in the universe out of its own substance. A Hindu, therefore, does not think it a sin to worship rivers, mountains, heavenly bodies, creatures, etc., since they are all consubstantial with God and manifestations of the same spirit. Any one of these manifestations may be selected to be the object of devotion, according to a man's own choice; his favorite divinity he will call the supreme ruler of the universe, and the others gods, servants of the supreme ruler.

Hindus believe in the immortality of the soul, inasmuch as it is consubstantial with God; man is rewarded or punished according to his deeds. He undergoes existences of different descriptions in order to reap the fruit of his deeds. When at length he is free from the consequences of his action, which he can be by knowing the Great Spirit as it is and its relation to himself, he is then re-absorbed into the spirit and ceases to be an individual; just as a river ceases to be different from the ocean when it flows into the sea.

According to this doctrine, a man is liable to be born eight million four hundred thousand times before he can become a Brahman (first caste), and except one be a Brahman he is not fit to be re-absorbed into the spirit, even though he obtain the true knowledge of the Paramatma. It is, therefore, necessary for every person of other castes to be careful not to transgress the law by any imprudent act, lest he be again subjected to be born eight million four hundred thousand times. A Brahman must incessantly try to attain to the perfection of the supreme knowledge, for it is his last chance to get rid of the misery of the long series of earthly existences; the least trifling transgression of social or religious rules however renders him liable to the degradation of perpetual births and deaths.

These, with the caste beliefs, are the chief articles of the Hindu creed at the present day. There are a few heterodox Hindus who deny all this; they are pure theists in their belief, and disregard all idolatrous customs. These Bramos, as they are called, are doing much good by purifying the national religion.

As regards social customs, it may be said that the daily life and habits of the people are immensely influenced by religion in India. There is not an act that is not performed religiously by them; a humorous author has said, with some truth, that "the Hindus even sin religiously." The rising from the bed in the morning, the cleaning of teeth, washing of hands and bathing of the body, the wear-

Prefatory Remarks.

ing of garments, lighting the fire or the lamp, eating and drinking and every act of similar description, is done in a prescribed manner, and with the utterance of prayers or in profound silence. Each custom, when it is old enough to be entitled "the way of the ancients," takes the form of religion and is scrupulously observed. These customs, founded for the most part on tradition, are altogether independent of the canonical writings, so much so that a person is liable to be punished, or even excommunicated, for doing a deed forbidden by custom, even though it be sanctioned by religion.

For example, eating the food prepared by persons of an inferior caste is not only not forbidden by the sacred laws, but is sanctioned by them.*

At the present day, however, time-honored

---

* "Pure men of the first three castes shall prepare the food of a householder" (Brahman or other high caste).

"Or Shudras (servile caste) may prepare the food under the superintendence of men of the first three castes."— *Apastamba* II. 2, 3. 1. 4.

custom overrules the ancient laws, and says that a person must not eat anything cooked nor drink water polluted by the touch of a person of inferior caste. Hindus transgressing this rule instantly forfeit their caste, and must undergo some heavy penance to regain it.

Without doubt, "caste" originated in the economical division of labor. The talented and most intelligent portion of the Aryan Hindus became, as was natural, the governing body of the entire race. They, in their wisdom, saw the necessity of dividing society, and subsequently set each portion apart to undertake certain duties which might promote the welfare of the nation. The priesthood (Brahman caste) were appointed to be the spiritual governors over all, and were the recognized head of society. The vigorous, warlike portion of the people (Kshatriya, or warrior caste) was to defend the country, and suppress crime and injustice by means of physical strength; assisted by the priesthood, they were to be the temporal governors in the administration of justice. The business-loving tradesmen and artisans (Vaisya, or trader caste) had also an important position assigned under the preceding classes or castes. The fourth, or servile class (Shudra caste) was made up of all those not included in the preceding three castes. In ancient times persons were assigned to each of the four castes according to their individual capacity and merit, independent of the accident of birth.

Later on, when caste became an article of the Hindu faith, it assumed the formidable proportions which now prevail everywhere in India. A son of a Brahman is honored as the head of all castes, not because of his merit, but because he was born into a Brahman family. Intermarriage of castes was once recognized as lawful, even after caste by inheritance had been acknowledged, provided that a woman of superior caste did not marry a man of an inferior caste; but now law is overruled by custom. Intermarriages cannot take place without involving serious consequences, and making the offenders outcasts.

The four principal castes* are again divided into clans; men belonging to high clans must not give their daughters in marriage to men of low clans. To transgress this custom is to lose family honor, caste privileges, and even intercourse with friends and relatives.

Besides the four castes and their clans there are numerous castes called collectively, "mixed castes" formed by the intermarriage of members of the preceding; their number is again increased by castes according to employment, as scribe, tanner, cobbler, shoemaker, tailor, etc., etc. Even the outcasts, such for example as the sweeper, have their own distinctions, as powerful among themselves as are

---

* "There are four castes—Brahmanas, Kshatriyas, Vaisyas, and Shudras."

"Amongst these, each preceding caste is superior by birth to the one following."—*Apastamba* I. 1, 1, 3, 4.

"The Brahmana, the Kshatriya and the Vaisya castes are the twice-born ones, but the fourth, the Shudra, has one birth only; there is no fifth caste."—*Manu* X. 4.

those of the high castes. Transgressors of caste rules are, from the highest to the lowest, subject to excommunication and severe punishment. Offenders by intermarriage, or change of faith, are without redemption. It must also be borne in mind, that if a Brahman condescends to marry a person of lower caste, or eats and drinks with any of them, he is despised and shunned as an outcast, not only by his own caste, but also by the low-caste with whose members he has entered into such relation. The low-caste people will look upon this Brahman as a lawless wretch. So deeply rooted is this custom in the heart of every orthodox Hindu that he is not in any way offended by the disrespect shown him by a high caste man, since he recognizes in it only what is ordered by religion. For, although "caste" is confessedly an outgrowth of social order, it has now become the first great article of the Hindu creed all over India. Thoughtful men like Buddha, Nanak, Chaitanya and others rebelled against this tyrannical custom, and proclaimed the gospel of social equality of all men, but "caste" proved too strong for them. Their disciples at the present day are as much subject to caste as are any other orthodox Hindus. Even the Mahomedans have not escaped this tyrant; they, too, are divided into several castes, and are as strict as the Hindus in their observances. Over a million Hindu converts to Christianity, members of the Roman Catholic Church, are more or less ruled by caste. The Protestant missionaries, likewise, found it difficult in early days to overcome caste prejudice among their converts, and not many years ago, in the Madras presidency, clergymen were compelled to use different cups for each separate caste when they celebrated the Lord's Supper.

The Vedas are believed by the devout Hindu to be the eternal, self-existing Word of God, revealed by Him to different sages. Besides the Vedas there are more than twenty-five books of sacred law, ascribed to different

Prefatory Remarks.

inspired authors who wrote or compiled them at various times, and on which are based the principal customs and religious institutes of the Hindus. Among these, the code of Manu ranks highest, and is believed by all to be very sacred, second to none but the Vedas themselves.

Although Manu and the other law-givers differ greatly on many points, they all agree on things concerning women. According to this sacred law a woman's life is divided into three parts, viz :—1st, Childhood ; 2nd, Youth or married life ; 3rd, Widowhood or old age.

NOTE.—*The translations of the sacred texts quoted throughout this work are those found in the well-known " Sacred Books of the East," edited by Prof. Max Müller, Clarendon Press, Oxford.*

CHAPTER II.

CHILDHOOD.

ALTHOUGH the code of Manu contains a single passage in which it is written "A daughter is equal to a son," (See Manu ix., 130), the context expressly declares that equality to be founded upon the results attainable through her son; the passage therefore cannot be regarded as an exception to the statement that the ancient code establishes the superiority of male children. A son is the most coveted of all blessings that a Hindu craves, for it is by a son's birth in the family that the father is redeemed.

"Through a son he conquers the worlds, through a

son's son he obtains immortality, but through his son's grandson he gains the world of the sun."—*Manu*, ix., 137.

"There is no place for a man (in Heaven) who is destitute of male offspring."—*Vasishtha*, xvii. 2.

If a man is sonless, it is desirable that he should have a daughter, for her *son* stands in the place of a son to his grandfather, through whom the grandfather may obtain salvation.

"Between a son's son and the son of a daughter there exists in this world no difference; for even the son of a daughter saves him who has no sons, in the next world, like the son's son."—*Manu*, ix. 139.

In Western and Southern India when a girl or a woman salutes the elders and priests, they bless her with these words—"Mayst thou have eight sons, and may thy husband survive thee." In the form of a blessing the deity is never invoked to grant daughters. Fathers very seldom wish to have daughters, for they are thought to be the property of somebody else; besides, a daughter is not supposed to be of any use to the parents in their old age. Although it is necessary for the continuance of the race that some girls should be born into the world, it is desirable that their number by no means should exceed that of the boys. If unfortunately a wife happens to have all daughters and no son, Manu authorizes the husband of such a woman to supersede her with another in the eleventh year of their marriage.*

In no other country is the mother so laden with care and anxiety on the approach of childbirth as in India. In most cases her hope of winning her husband to herself hangs solely on her bearing sons.

Women of the poorest as well as of the richest families, are almost invariably subjected to this trial. Many are the sad and heart-rending stories heard from the lips of unhappy women who have lost their husband's favor by bringing forth daughters only, or by having no children at all. Never shall I forget a sorrowful scene that I witnessed in my childhood. When about thirteen years of age

---

* See page 61.

I accompanied my mother and sister to a royal harem where they had been invited to pay a visit. The Prince had four wives, three of whom were childless. The eldest having been blessed with two sons, was of course the favorite of her husband, and her face beamed with happiness.

We were shown into the nursery and the royal bed-chamber, where signs of peace and contentment were conspicuous. But oh! what a contrast to this brightness was presented in the apartments of the childless three. Their faces were sad and careworn; there seemed no hope for them in this world, since their lord was displeased with them, on account of their misfortune.

A lady friend of mine in Calcutta told me that her husband had warned her not to give birth to a girl, the first time, or he would never see her face again, but happily for this wife and for her husband also, she had two sons before the daughter came. In the same family there was another woman, the sister-in-law of my friend, whose first-born had been a daughter. She longed unceasingly to have a son, in order to win her husband's favor, and when I went to the house, constantly besought me to foretell whether this time she should have a son! Poor woman! she had been notified by her husband that if she persisted in bearing daughters she should be superseded by another wife, have coarse clothes to wear and scanty food to eat, should have no ornaments, save those which are necessary to show the existence of a husband, and she should be made the drudge of the whole household. Not unfrequently, it is asserted, that bad luck attends a girl's advent, and poor superstitious mothers in order to avert such a catastrophe, attempt to convert the unborn child into a boy, if unhappily it be a girl.

Rosaries used by mothers of sons are procured to pray with; herbs and roots celebrated for their virtue are eagerly and regularly swallowed; trees and son-giving gods are devoutly worshipped. There is a curious ceremony, honored with the name of "sacrament," which is administered to the mother between the third and the fourth month of her pregnancy for the purpose of converting the embryo into a boy.

In spite of all these precautions girls will come into Hindu households as ill-luck, or rather nature, will have it. After the birth of one or more sons girls are not unwelcome, and under such circumstances, mothers very often long to have a daughter. And after her birth both parents lavish love and tenderness upon her, for natural affection, though modified and blunted by cruel custom, is still strong in the parent's heart. Especially may this be the case with the Hindu *mother*. That maternal affection, sweet and strong, before which "there is neither male nor female," asserts itself not unfrequently in Hindu homes, and overcomes selfishness and false fear of popular custom. A loving mother will sacrifice her own happiness by braving the displeasure of her lord, and will treat her little daughter as the best of all treasures. Such heroism is truly praiseworthy in a woman; any country might be proud of her. But alas! the dark side is too conspicuous to be passed over in silence.

In a home shadowed by adherence to cruel custom and prejudice, a child is born into the world; the poor mother is greatly distressed to learn that the little stranger is a daughter, and the neighbors turn their noses in all directions to manifest their disgust and indignation at the occurrence of such a phenomenon. The innocent babe is happily unconscious of all that is going on around her, for a time at least. The mother, who has lost the favor of her husband and relatives because of the girl's birth, may selfishly avenge herself by showing disregard to infantile needs and slighting babyish requests. Under such a mother the baby soon begins to *feel* her misery, although she does not understand how or why she is caused to suffer this cruel injustice.

If a girl is born after her brother's death,

or if, soon after her birth, a boy in the family dies, she is in either case regarded by her parents and neighbors as the cause of the boy's death. She is then constantly addressed with some unpleasant name, slighted, beaten, cursed, persecuted and despised by all. Strange to say, some parents, instead of thinking of her as a comfort left to them, find it in their hearts, in the constant manifestation of their grief for the dear lost boy, to address the innocent girl with words such as these: "Wretched girl, why didst thou not die instead of our darling boy? Why didst thou crowd him out of the house by coming to us; or why didst not thou thyself become a boy?" "It would have been good for all of us if thou hadst died and thy brother lived!" I have myself several times heard parents say such things to their daughters, who, in their turn, looked sadly and wonderingly into the parents' faces, not comprehending why such cruel speeches should be heaped upon their heads when they had not done any harm to their brothers.

If there is a boy remaining in the family, all the caresses and sweet words, the comforts and gifts, the blessings and praises are lavished upon him by parents and neighbors, and even by servants, who fully sympathize with the parents in their grief. On every occasion the poor girl is made to feel that she has no right to share her brother's good fortune, and that she is an unwelcome, unbidden guest in the family.

Brothers, in most cases, are, of course, very proud of their superior sex ; they can know no better than what they see and hear concerning their own and their sisters' qualities. They, too, begin by and by to despise girls and women. It is not a rare thing to hear a mere slip of a boy gravely lecture his elder sister as to what she should or should not do, and remind her that she is only a girl and that *he* is a *boy*. Subjected to such humiliation, most girls become sullen, morbid and dull. There are some fiery natures, however, who burn with indignation, and burst out in their own childish eloquence; they tell their brothers and cousins that they soon are going to be given in marriage, and that they will not come to see them, even if they are often entreated to do so. Children, however, soon forget the wrong done them; they laugh, they shout, they run about freely, and are generally merry when unpleasant speeches are not showered upon them. Having little or no education, except a few prayers and popular songs to commit to memory, the little girls are mostly left to themselves, and they play in whatever manner they please. When about six or seven years of age they usually begin to help their mothers in household work, or in taking care of the younger children.

I have mentioned earlier the strictness of the modern caste system in regard to marriage. Intelligent readers may, therefore, have already guessed that this reason lies at the bottom of the disfavor shown to girls in Hindu homes. From the first moment of the daughter's birth, the parents are tormented incessantly with anxiety in regard to her future, and the responsibilities of their position. Marriage is the most expensive of all Hindu festivities and ceremonies. The marriage of a girl of a high caste family involves an expenditure of two hundred dollars at the very least. Poverty in India is so great that not many fathers are able to incur this expense; if there are more than two daughters in a family, his ruin is inevitable. For, it should be remembered, the bread-winner of the house in Hindu society not only has to feed his own wife and children, but also his parents, his brothers unable to work either through ignorance or idleness, their families and the nearest widowed relatives, all of whom very often depend upon one man for their support; besides these, there are the family priests, religious beggars and others, who expect much from him. Thus, fettered hand and foot by barbarously cruel customs which threaten to strip him of everything he has, starvation and death staring him in the face, the wretched father of many girls is truly an object of pity. Religion enjoins that every girl must be given in marriage; the neglect of this duty means for the father unpardonable sin, public ridicule and caste excommunication. But this is not all. The girl must be married within a fixed period, the caste of the future husband must be the same, and the clan either equal or superior, *but never inferior*, to that of her father.

The Brahmans of Eastern India have observed successfully their clan prejudice for hundreds of years despite poverty; they have done this in part by taking advantage of the custom of polygamy. A Brahman of a high clan will marry ten, eleven, twenty, or even one hundred and fifty girls. He makes a business of it. He goes up and down the land marrying girls, receiving presents from their parents, and immediately thereafter bidding good-bye to the brides; going home, he never returns to them. The illustrious Brahman need not bother himself with the care of supporting so many wives, for the parents pledge themselves to maintain the daughter all her life, if she stays with them a married virgin to the end. In case of such a marriage as this, the father is not required to spend money beyond his means, nor is it difficult for him to support the daughter, for she is useful to the family in doing the cooking and other household work; moreover, the father has the satisfaction *first*, of having given his daughter in marriage, and thereby having escaped disgrace and the ridicule of society; *secondly*, of having obtained for himself the bright mansions of the gods, since his daughter's husband is a Brahman of high clan.

But this form of polygamy does not exist among the Kshatriyas, because, as a member of the non-Brahman caste, a man is not allowed by religion, to beg or to receive gifts from others, except from friends; he therefore cannot support either many wives or many daughters. Caste and clan prejudice tyrannized the Rajputs of North and Northwestern and Central India, who belong to the Kshatriyas or warrior caste, to such an extent that they were driven to introduce the inhuman and irreligious custom of female infanticide into their society. This cruel act was performed by the fathers themselves, or even by mothers, at the command of the husband whom they are bound to obey in *all* things.

It is a universal custom among the Rajputs for neighbors and friends to assemble to congratulate the father upon the birth of a child. If a boy is born, his birth is announced with music, glad songs and by distributing sweetmeats. If a daughter, the father coolly announces that "nothing" has been born into his family, by which expression it is understood that the child is a girl, and that she is very likely to be *nothing* in this world, and the friends go home grave and quiet.

After considering how many girls could safely be allowed to live, the father took good care to defend himself from caste and clan tyranny by killing the extra girls at birth, which was as easily accomplished as destroying a mosquito or other annoying insect. Who can save a babe if the parents are determined to slay her, and eagerly watch for a suitable opportunity? Opium is generally used to keep the crying child quiet, and a small pill of this drug is sufficient to accomplish the cruel task; a skillful pressure upon the neck, which is known as the "putting nail to the throat," also answers the purpose. There are several other nameless methods that may be employed in sacrificing the innocents upon the unholy altar of the caste and clan system. Then there are not a few child-thieves who generally steal girls; even the wild animals are so intelligent and of such refined taste that they mock at British law, and almost always steal girls to satisfy their hunger.

Female infanticide, though not sanctioned by religion, and never looked upon as right by conscientious people, has, nevertheless, in those parts of India mentioned, been silently passed over unpunished by society in general.

As early as 1802 the British government

enacted laws for the suppression of this horrid crime ; and more than forty years ago Major Ludlow, a kind-hearted Englishman, induced the semi-independent States to prohibit this custom, which the Hindu princes did, by a mutual agreement not to allow any one to force the father of a girl to give more dowry than his circumstances should warrant, and to discourage extravagance in the celebration of marriages. But caste and clan prejudice could not be overcome so easily.

Large expenses might be stopped by law, but a belief, deeply rooted in the hearts and religiously observed by the people for centuries, could not be removed by external rules.

The Census of 1870 revealed the curious fact that three hundred children were stolen in one year by wolves from within the city of Umritzar, all the children being girls, and this under the very nose of the English government. In the year 1868 an English official, Mr. Hobart, made a tour of inspection through those parts of India where female infanticide was most practiced before the government enacted the prohibitory law. As a result of careful observation, he came to the conclusion that this horrible practice was still followed in secret, and to an alarming extent.

The Census returns of 1880-81 show that there are fewer women than men in India by over five millions. Chief among the causes which have brought about this surprising numerical difference of the sexes may be named, after female infanticide in certain parts of the country, *the imperfect treatment of the diseases of women in all parts of Hindustan, together with lack of proper hygienic care and medical attendance.*

CHAPTER III.

MARRIED LIFE.

It is not easy to determine when the childhood of a Hindu girl ends and the married life begins. The early marriage system, although not the oldest custom of my country, is at least five hundred years older than the Christian era. According to Manu, eight years is the minimum, and twelve years of age the maximum marriageable age for a high caste girl.* The earlier the act of giving the daughter in marriage, the greater is the merit, for thereby the parents are entitled to rich rewards in heaven.

---

*A man aged thirty years shall marry a maiden of twelve who pleases him, or a man of twenty-four a girl of eight years of age.—*Manu* ix., 94.

There have always been exceptions to this rule, however. Among the eight kinds of marriages described in the law, there is one form that is only an agreement between the lovers to be loyal to each other; in this form of marriage there is no religious ceremony, nor even a third party to witness and confirm the agreement and relationship, and yet by the law this is regarded as completely lawful a marriage as any other. It is quite plain from this fact that all girls were not betrothed between the age of eight and twelve years, and also that marriage was not considered a religious institution by the Hindus in olden times. All castes and classes could marry in this form if they chose to do so. One of the most noticeable facts connected with this form is this: women as well as men were quite free to choose their own future spouses. In Europe and America women do choose their husbands, but it is considered a shame for a woman to be the first to request marriage, and both men and women will be shocked equally at such an occurrence; but in India, women had equal freedom with men, in this case at least. A woman might, without being put to shame, and without shocking the other party, come forward and select her own husband. The Svayamvara (selecting husband) was quite common until as late as the eleventh century, A. D., and even now, although very rarely, this custom is practiced by a few people.

I know of a woman in the Bombay presidency who is married to a Brahman according to this form. The first wife of the man is still living; the second wife, being of another caste, he could not openly acknowledge as his religiously wedded wife, but he could do so without going through the religious ceremony had she been of his own caste, as the act is sanctioned by Hindu law. The lawless behaviour of the Mahomedan intruders from the twelfth century, A. D., had much to do in universalizing infant marriage in India. A great many girls are given in marriage at the present day literally while they are still in their cradles; from five to eleven years is the usual period for their marriage among the Brahmans all over India. As it is absurd to assume that girls should be allowed to choose their future husbands in their infancy, this is done for them by their parents and guardians. In the northern part of the country the family barber is generally employed to select boys and girls to be married, it being considered too humiliating and mean an act on the part of parents and guardians to go out to seek their future daughters and sons-in-law.

Although Manu has distinctly said that twenty-four years is the minimum marriageable age for a young man, the popular custom defies the law. Boys of ten and twelve are now doomed to be married to girls of seven and eight years of age. A boy of a well-to-do family does not generally remain a bachelor after seventeen or eighteen years of age; the respectable but very poor families, even if they are of high caste, cannot afford to marry their boys so soon, but even among them it is a shame for a man to remain unmarried after twenty or twenty-five. Boys as well as girls have no voice in the selection of their spouses at the first marriage, but if a man lose his first wife, and marries a second time, *he* has a voice in the matter.

Although the ancient law-givers thought it desirable to marry girls when quite young, and consequently ignored their right to choose their own husbands, yet they were not altogether void of humane feelings. They have positively forbidden parents and guardians to give away girls in marriage unless good suitors were offered them.

"To a distinguished, handsome suitor of equal caste should a father give his daughter in accordance with the prescribed rule, though she have not attained the proper age."—*Manu* ix., 88.

"But the maiden, though marriageable, should rather stop in the father's house until death, than that he should ever give her to a man destitute of good qualities."—*Manu*, ix. 89.

But, alas, here too the law is defied by cruel custom. It allows some men to remain unmarried, but woe to the maiden and to her family if she is so unfortunate as to remain single after the marriageable age. Although no law has ever said so, the popular belief is that a woman can have no salvation unless she be formally married. It is not, then, a matter of wonder that parents become extremely anxious when their daughters are over eight or nine and are unsought in marriage. Very few suitors offer to marry the daughters of poor parents, though they may be of high caste families. Wealth has its own pride and merit in India, as everywhere else in the world, but even this powerful wealth is as nothing before caste rule. A high caste man will never condescend to marry his daughter to a low caste man though he be a millionaire.

But wealth in one's own caste surpasses the merits of learning, beauty and honor; parents generally seek boys of well-to-do families for their sons-in-law. As the boys are too young to pass as possessing "good qualities," *i. e.*, learning, common-sense, ability to support and take care of a family, and respectable character, the parents wish to see their daughter safe in a family where she will, at least, have plenty to eat and to wear; they, of course, wish her to be happy with her husband, but in their judgment that is not the one thing needful. So long as *they* have fulfilled the custom, and thereby secured a good name in this world and heavenly reward in the next, their minds are not much troubled concerning the girl's fate. If the boy be of rich or middle class people, a handsome sum of money must be given to him and his family in order to secure the marriage; beside this, the girl's family must walk very humbly with this little god, for he is believed to be indwelt by the god Vishnu. Poor parents cannot have the advantage of marrying their daughters to boys of prosperous families, and as they *must* marry them to some one, it very frequently happens that girls of eight or nine are given to men of sixty and seventy, or to men utterly unworthy of the young maidens.

Parents who have the means to secure good-looking, prosperous men for their sons-in-law, take great care to consult the horoscopes of both parties in order to know the future of their daughters; in such cases, they are anxious to ascertain, over and above all things, that the girl shall not become a widow. If the daughter's horoscope reveals that her future husband is to survive her, the match is considered very satisfactory; but if it reveals the reverse, then a boy having a horoscope equally bad is sought for, because it is sincerely believed that in that case the guardian planets will wrestle with each other, and, as almost always happens, that the stronger, *i. e.*, the husband's planet will be victorious, or else both parties will fall in the conflict, and the husband and wife die together. A friend of mine informed me that three hundred horoscopes were rejected before one was found which agreed satisfactorily with her sister's guardian planet. Undoubtedly many suitors, who might make good husbands for these little girls, are for this reason rejected, and unworthy men fall to their lot; thus, the horoscope becomes a source of misery instead of blessing.

It not unfrequently happens that fathers give away their daughters in marriage to strangers without exercising care in making inquiry concerning the suitor's character and social position. It is enough to learn from the man's own statement, his caste and clan, and the locality of his home. I know of a most extraordinary marriage that took place in the following manner: the father was on a religious pilgrimage with his family, which consisted of his wife and two daughters, one nine and the other seven years of age, and they had stopped in a town to take rest for a day or two. One morning the father was bathing in the sacred river Godavari, near the town, when he saw a fine-looking man coming to bathe there also. After the ablution and the morning prayers were over, the father inquired of the stranger who he was and whence he came; on learning his caste, and clan, and dwelling-place, also that he was a widower, the father offered him his little daughter of nine, in marriage. All things were settled in an hour or so; next day the marriage was concluded, and the little girl placed in the possession of the stranger, who took her nearly nine hundred miles away from her home. The father left the place the day after the marriage without the daughter, and pursued his pilgrimage with a light heart; fortunately the little girl had fallen in good hands, and was well and tenderly cared for beyond all expectation, but the conduct of her father, who cared so little to ascertain his daughter's fate, is none the less censurable.

When the time to conclude the marriage ceremony draws near, the Hindu mother's affection for the girl frequently knows no bounds; she indulges her in endless ways, knowing that in a few days her darling will be torn away from her loving embrace. When she goes to pay the customary visit to her child's future mother-in-law many are the tearful entreaties and soul-stirring solicitations that she will be as kind and forbearing toward the little stranger as though she were her own daughter. The boy's mother is moved at this time, for she has a woman's heart, and she promises to be a mother to the little bride. On the day fixed for the marriage, parents formally give their daughter away to the boy; afterwards the young people are united by priests who utter the sacred texts and pronounce them man and wife in the presence of the sacred fire and of relatives and friends. The marriage being thus concluded, it is henceforth indissoluble.

"Neither by sale nor by repudiation is a wife released from her husband; such we know the law to be which the Lord of creatures made of old."—*Manu* ix., 46.

Marriage is the only "Sacrament" administered to a high caste woman, accompanied with the utterance of the Vedic texts. It is to be presumed that the texts are introduced in honor of the man whom she marries, for no sacrament must be administered to him without the sacred formulæ. Henceforth the girl is his, not only his property, but also that of his nearest relatives.

"For they (the ancient sages) declare that a bride is given to the family of her husband, and not to the husband alone."—*Apastamba II.*, 10, 27, 3.

The girl now belongs to the husband's clan; she is known by his family name, and in some parts of India the husband's relatives will not allow her to be called by the first name that was given her by her parents; henceforth she is a kind of impersonal being. She can have no merit or quality of her own.

"Whatever be the qualities of the man with whom a woman is united in lawful marriage, such qualities even she assumes, like a river united with the ocean."—*Manu* ix., 22.

Many of our girls when asked in fun whether they would like soon to be married would innocently answer in the affirmative. They often see their sisters, cousins or playmates married; the occasion is one long to be remembered with pleasure. Even the poorest families take great pains to make it pleasant to everybody; children enjoy it most of all. There are gorgeous dresses, bright colored clothes, beautiful decorations, music, songs, fireworks, fun, plenty of fruit and sweet things to eat and to give away, lovely flowers, and the whole house is illuminated with many lamps. What can be more tempting to a child's mind than these? In addition to all this the big elephant is sometimes brought, on which the newly-married children ride in procession amidst all sorts of fun. Is it not grand enough for a child? Oh, I shall ride on the back of the elephant! thinks the girl; and there is something more besides; all the people in the house will wait on me, will make much of me; everybody will caress and try to please me. "Oh, what fun!"

"I like to have a cold, and be ill," said a girl of four. "Why, darling?" asked her mother, in surprise. "Oh, because," replied the little girl, "I like to eat my breakfast in bed, and then, too, everybody waits on me!"

Who has not heard remarks such as these, and laughed heartily over them? Children like even to be ill for the sake of being waited on.

What wonder, then, if Hindu girls like being married for the sake of enjoying that much-coveted privilege! But little do these poor innocents know what comes after the fun. Little do they imagine that they must bid farewell to home and mother, to noisy merriment, and laughter, and to the free life of pure enjoyment. Sometimes the child desires to be married when, through superstition, she is ill-treated at home by her nearest relatives, otherwise there can be no reason except the enjoyment of fun that excites the desire in the girl's heart, for when the marriage takes place she is just emerging from babyhood.

Childhood is, indeed, the heyday of a Hindu woman's life. Free to go in and out where she pleases, never bothered by caste or other social restrictions, never worried by lesson-learning, sewing, mending or knitting, loved, petted and spoiled by parents, brothers and sisters, uncles and aunts, she is little different from a young colt whose days are spent in complete liberty. Then lo, all at once the ban of marriage is pronounced and the yoke put on her neck forever!

Immediately after the marriage ceremony is concluded the boy takes his girl-bride home and delivers her over to his own mother, who becomes from that time until the girl grows old enough to be given to her husband, her sole mistress, and who wields over the daughter-in-law undisputed authority!

It must be borne in mind that both in Northern and Southern India, the term "marriage" does not mean anything more than an irrevocable betrothal. The ceremony gone through at that time establishes *religiously* the conjugal relationship of both parties; there is a second ceremony that confirms the relationship both religiously and socially, which does not take place until the children attain the age of puberty. In Bengal the rule is somewhat different, and proves in many cases greatly injurious to the human system. In some very rare cases the girls are allowed to remain with their own parents for a time at least. In the

North of India the little bride's lot is a happier one to begin with; she not being forced to go to her husband's home until she is about thirteen or fourteen years of age.

The joint family system, which is one of the peculiarities of Eastern countries, is very deeply rooted in the soil of India. There may not unfrequently be found four generations living under one roof. The house is divided into two distinct parts, namely, the outer and the inner court. The houses, as a rule, have but few windows, and they are usually dark; the men's court is comparatively light and good. Houses in country places are better than those in the crowded cities. Men and women have almost nothing in common.

The women's court is situated at the back of the house, where darkness reigns perpetually. There the child-bride is brought to be forever confined. She does not enter her husband's house to be the head of a new home, but rather enters the house of the father-in-law to become the lowest of its members, and to occupy the humblest position in the family. Breaking the young bride's spirits is an essential part of the discipline of this new abode. She must never talk or laugh loudly, must never speak before or to the father and elder brother-in-law, or any other distant male relatives of her husband, unless commanded to do so. In Northern India, where all women wear veils, the young bride or woman covers her face with it, or runs into another room to show respect to them, when these persons enter an apartment where she happens to be. In Southern India, where women, as a rule, do not wear veils, they need not cover their faces; they rise to show respect to elders and to their husbands, and remain standing as long as they are obliged to be in their presence.

The mothers-in-law employ their daughters in all kinds of household work, in order to give them a thorough knowledge of domestic duties. These children of nine or ten years of age find it irksome to work hard all day long without the hope of hearing a word of praise from the mother-in-law. As a rule, the little girl is scolded for every mistake she commits; if the work be well done, it is silently accepted, words of encouragement and praise from the elders being regarded as spoiling children and demoralizing them; the faults of the little ones are often mistaken for intentional offences, and then the artillery of abusive speech is opened upon them; thus, mortified and distressed, they seek to console themselves by shedding bitter tears in silence. In such sorrowful hours they miss the dear mother and her loving sympathy.

I must, however, do justice to the mothers-in-law. Many of them treat the young brides of their sons as their own children; many are kind and affectionate, but ignorant; they easily lose their temper and seem to be hard when they do not mean to be so. Others again, having themselves been the victims of merciless treatment in their childhood become hard-hearted; such an one will do all she can to torment the child by using abusive language, by beating her and slandering her before the neighbors. Often she is not satisfied by doing this herself, but induces and encourages the son to join her. I have several times seen young wives shamefully beaten by beastly young husbands who cherished no natural love for them.

As we have seen, the marriage is concluded without the consent of either party, and after it the bride is not allowed to speak or be acquainted with the husband until after the second ceremony, and even then the young couple must never betray any sign of their mutual attachment before a third party. Under such circumstances they seldom meet and talk; it may therefore be easily understood that being cut off from the chief means of forming attachment, the young couple are almost strangers, and in many cases do not like their relationship; and if in the midst of all this, the mother-in-law begins to encourage the young man to torment his wife in various ways, it is not strange that a feeling akin to hatred takes root between them. A child of thirteen was cruelly beaten by her husband in my presence for telling the simple truth, that she did not like so well to be in his house as at her own home.

In spite, however, of all these drawbacks, there is in India many a happy and loving couple that would be an honor to any nation. Where the conjugal relation is brightened by mutual love, the happy wife has nothing to complain of except the absence of freedom of thought and action; but since wives have never known from the beginning what freedom is, they are generally well content to remain in bondage; there is, however, no such thing as the family having pleasant times together.

Men spend their evenings and other leisure hours with friends of their own sex, either in the outer court or away from home. Children enjoy the company of father and mother alternately, by going in and out when they choose, but the children of young parents are never made happy by the father's caresses or any other demonstration of his love in the presence of the elders; the notion of false moddesty prevents the young father from speaking to his children freely. The women of the family usually take their meals after the men have had theirs, and the wife, as a rule, eats what her lord may please to leave on his plate.

CHAPTER IV.

WOMAN'S PLACE IN RELIGION AND SOCIETY.

THE Hindu religion commands ;

"Women must be honored and adorned by their fathers, brothers, husbands, and brothers-in-law, who desire their own welfare."

"Where women are honored, there the gods are pleased ; but where they are not honored, no sacred rite yields rewards."

"Where the female relations live in grief, the family soon wholly perishes; but that family where they are not unhappy ever prospers."

"The houses on which female relations, not being duly honored, pronounce a curse, perish completely, as if destroyed by magic."

"Hence men who seek their own welfare, should always honor women on holidays and festivals with (gifts of) ornaments, clothes and dainty food."

"In that family where the husband is pleased with his

wife, and the wife with her husband, happiness will assuredly be lasting."

"For if the wife is not radiant with beauty, she will not attract her husband; but if she has no attractions for him, no children will be born."

"If the wife is radiant with beauty, the whole house is bright; but if she is destitute of beauty, all will appear dismal."—*Manu*, iii., 55–62.

These commandments are very significant. Our Aryan Hindus did, and still do honor woman to a certain extent. The honor bestowed upon the *mother* is without parallel in any other country. Although the woman is looked upon as an inferior being, the mother is nevertheless the chief person and worthy to receive all honor from the son. One of the great commandments of the Hindu Scriptures is, "Let thy mother be to thee like unto a god."*

---

* My readers would perhaps be interested to see these commandments; they are as follows:—"After having taught the Veda, the teacher instructs the pupil:

Say what is true.

Do thy duty.

Do not neglect the study of the Veda.

The mother is the queen of the son's household. She wields great power there, and is generally obeyed as the head of the family by her sons and by her daughters-in-law.

But there is a reverse side to the shield that should not be left unobserved. This is best studied in the laws of Manu, as all Hindus, with a few exceptions believe implicitly what that law-giver says about women:

After having brought to thy teacher his proper reward, do not cut off the line of children! (*i. e.* Do not remain unmarried).

Do not swerve from the truth.

Do not swerve from duty.

Do not neglect what is useful.

Do not neglect the learning and teaching of the Veda.

Do not neglect the sacrificial works due to the gods and fathers.

Let thy mother be to thee like unto a god.

Let thy father be to thee like unto a god.

Let thy teacher be to thee like unto a god.

Let thy guests be to thee like unto a god.

Whatever actions are blameless those should be regarded, not others.

Whatever good works have been performed by us, should be observed by thee, not others."—*Taittiriya Upanishad*, Valli, i. An. xi., 1, 2.

In Religion and Society. 53

"It is the nature of women to seduce men in this world; for that reason the wise are never unguarded in the company of females."

"For women are able to lead astray in this world not only a fool, but even a learned man, and to make him a slave of desire and anger."—*Manu*, ii., 213-214.

"Women do not care for beauty, nor is their attention fixed on age; thinking 'it is enough that he is a man,' they give themselves to the handsome and to the ugly."

"Through their passion for men, through their mutable temper, through their natural heartlessness, they become disloyal towards their husbands, however carefully they may be guarded in this world."

"Knowing their disposition, which the Lord of creatures laid in them at the creation, to be such, every man should most strenuously exert himself to guard them."

"When creating them, Manu allotted to women a love of their bed, of their seat and of ornament, impure desires, wrath, dishonesty, malice and bad conduct."

"For women no sacramental rite is performed with sacred texts, thus the law is settled; women who are destitute of strength and destitute of the knowledge of Vedic texts, are as impure as falsehood itself, that is a fixed rule."—*Manu* ix., 14-18.

Such is the opinion of Manu concerning all women; and all men with more or less faith in the law regard women, even though they be their own mothers, "as impure as falsehood itself."

"And to this effect many sacred texts are chanted also in the Vedas, in order to make fully known the true disposition of women; hear now those texts which refer to the expiation of their sins."

"'If my mother, going astray and unfaithful, conceived illicit desires, may my father keep that seed from me,' that is the scriptural text."—*Manu* ix., 19, 20.

Such distrust and such low estimate of woman's nature and character in general, is at the root of the custom of seclusion of women in India. This mischievous custom has greatly increased and has become intensely tyrannical since the Mahomedan invasion; but that it existed from about the sixth century, B.C., cannot be denied. All male relatives are commanded by the law to deprive the women of the household of all their freedom:—

"Day and night women must be kept in dependence by the males of their families, and if they attach themselves to sensual enjoyments, they must be kept under one's control."

"Her father protects her in childhood, her husband protects her in youth, and her sons protect her in old age; a woman is never fit for independence."—*Manu* ix., 2, 3.

"Women must particularly be guarded against evil inclinations, however trifling they may appear; for if they are not guarded, they will bring sorrow on two families."

"Considering that the highest duty of all castes, even weak husbands must strive to guard their wives."—*Manu* ix., 5, 6.

"No man can completely guard women by force; but they can be guarded by the employment of the following expedients:"

"Let the husband employ his wife in the collection and expenditure of his wealth, in keeping everything clean, in the fulfilment of religious duties, in the preparation of his food, and in looking after the household utensils."—*Manu* ix., 10, 11.

Those who diligently and impartially read Sanscrit literature in the original, cannot fail to recognize the law-giver Manu as one of those hundreds who have done their best to make woman a hateful being in the world's eye. To employ her in housekeeping and kindred occupations is thought to be the only means of keeping her out of mischief, the blessed enjoyment of literary culture being denied her. She is forbidden to read the sacred scriptures, she has no right to pronounce a single syllable out of them. To appease her uncultivated, low kind of desire by giving her ornaments to adorn her person, and by giving her dainty food together with an occasional bow which costs nothing, are the highest honors to which a Hindu woman is entitled. She, the loving mother of the nation, the devoted wife, the tender sister and affectionate daughter is never fit for independence, and is "as impure as falsehood itself." She is never to be trusted; matters of importance are never to be committed to her.

I can say honestly and truthfully, that I have never read any sacred book in Sanscrit literature without meeting this kind of hateful sentiment about women. True, they contain here and there a kind word about them, but such words seem to me a heartless mockery after having charged them, as a class, with crime and evil deeds.

Profane literature is by no means less severe or more respectful towards women. I quote from the ethical teachings, parts of a catechism and also a few proverbs :—

Q. What is cruel?
A. The heart of a viper.
Q. What is more cruel than that?
A. The heart of a woman.
Q. What is the cruelest of all?
A. The heart of a sonless, penniless widow.

A catechism on moral subjects written by a Hindu gentleman of high literary reputation says:—

Q. What is the chief gate to hell?
A. A woman.
Q. What bewitches like wine?
A. A woman.
Q. Who is the wisest of the wise?
A. He who has not been deceived by women who may be compared to malignant fiends.
Q. What are fetters to men?
A. Women.
Q. What is that which cannot be trusted?
A. Women.
Q. What poison is that which appears like nectar?
A. Women.

PROVERBS.

"Never put your trust in women."

"Women's counsel leads to destruction."

"Woman is a great whirlpool of suspicion, a dwelling-place of vices, full of deceits, a hindrance in the way of heaven, the gate of hell."

Having fairly illustrated the popular belief about woman's nature, I now proceed to state woman's religion. Virtues such as truthfulness, forbearance, fortitude, purity of heart and uprightness, are common to men and women, but religion, as the word is commonly understood, has two distinct natures in the Hindu law; the masculine and the feminine. The masculine religion has its own peculiar duties, privileges and honors. The feminine religion also has its peculiarities.

The sum and substance of the latter may be given in a few words:—To look upon her husband as a god, to hope for salvation only through him, to be obedient to him in all things, never to covet independence, never to do anything but that which is approved by law and custom.

"Hear now the duties of women," says the law-giver, Manu:—

"By a girl, by a young woman, or even by an aged one, nothing must be done independently, even in her own house."

"In childhood, a female must be subject to her father, in youth, to her husband, when her lord is dead, to her sons; a woman must never be independent."

"She must not seek to separate herself from her father, husband, or sons; by leaving them she would make both her own and her husband's families contemptible."

"She must always be cheerful, clever in the management of her household affairs, careful in cleaning her utensils, and economical in expenditure."

"Him to whom her father may give her, or her brother with the father's permission, she shall obey as long as he lives, and when he is dead, she must not insult his memory."

"For the sake of procuring good fortune to brides, the recitation of benedictory texts, and the sacrifice to the Lord of creatures are used at weddings; but the betrothal by the father or guardian is the cause of the husband's dominion over his wife."

"The husband who wedded her with sacred texts, always gives happiness to his wife, both in season and out of season, in this world and in the next."

"Though destitute of virtue, or seeking pleasure elsewhere, or devoid of good qualities, yet a husband must be constantly worshipped as a god by a faithful wife."

"No sacrifice, no vow, no fast must be performed by women apart from their husbands; if a wife obeys her husband, she will for that reason alone, be exalted in heaven."

"A faithful wife, who desires to dwell after death with her husband, must never do anything that might displease him who took her hand whether he be alive or dead."—*Manu* v., 147–156.

"By violating her duty towards her husband, a wife is disgraced in this world, after death she enters the womb of a jackal, and is tormented by diseases, the punishment of her sin."

"She who, controlling her thoughts, words and deeds, never slights her lord, resides after death with her husband in heaven, and is called a virtuous wife."

"In reward of such conduct, a female who controls her thoughts, speech and actions, gains in this life highest renown, and in the next world a place near her husband."—*Manu* v., 164–166.

MARITAL RIGHTS.

"He only is a perfect man who consists of three persons united, his wife, himself and his offspring; thus says the Veda, and learned Brahmanas propound this maxim likewise, 'The husband is declared to be one with the wife.'"—*Manu* ix., 45.

The wife is declared to be the "marital property" of her husband, and is classed with "cows, mares, female camels, slave-girls, buffalo-cows, she-goats and ewes."—(See Manu ix., 48–51.)

The wife is punishable for treating her husband with aversion:—

"For one year let a husband bear with a wife who hates him; but after a lapse of a year, let him deprive her of her property and cease to live with her."

"She who shows disrespect to a husband who is addicted to some evil passion, is a drunkard, or diseased, shall be deserted for three months, and be deprived of her ornaments and furniture."—*Manu* ix., 77, 78.

"She who drinks spirituous liquor, is of bad conduct, rebellious, diseased, mischievous or wasteful, may at any time be superseded by another wife."

"A barren wife may be superseded in the eighth year, she whose children all die in the tenth, she who bears only daughters in the eleventh, but she who is quarrelsome without delay."—*Manu* ix., 80, 81.

"A wife who, being superseded, in anger departs from her husband's house, must either be instantly confined or cast off in the presence of the family."—*Manu* ix., 83.

"Though a man may have accepted a damsel in due form, he may abandon her if she be blemished or diseased, and if she have been given with fraud."—*Manu* ix., 72.

But no such provision is made for the woman; on the contrary, she must remain with and revere her husband as a god, even though he be destitute of virtue, or seek pleasure elsewhere, or devoid of good qualities, addicted to evil passion, fond of spirituous liquors or diseased, and what not!

How much impartial justice is shown in the treatment of womankind by Hindu law, can be fairly understood after reading the above quotations. In olden times these laws were enforced by the community; a husband had absolute power over his wife; she could do nothing but submit to his will without uttering a word of protest. Now, under the so-called Christian British rule, the woman is in no better condition than of old. True, the husband cannot as in the golden age, take her wherever she may be found, and drag her to his house, but his absolute power over her person has not suffered in the least. He is now bound to bring suit against her in the courts of justice to claim his "marital property," if she be unwilling to submit to him by any other means.

A near relative of mine had been given in her childhood in marriage to a boy whose parents agreed to let him stay and be educated with her in her own home. No sooner however, had the marriage ceremony been concluded than they forgot their agreement; the boy was taken to the home of his parents where he remained to grow up to be a worthless dunce, while his wife through the kindness and advanced views of her father, developed into a bright young woman and well accomplished.

Thirteen years later, the young man came to claim his wife, but the parents had no heart to send their darling daughter with a beggar who possessed neither the power nor the sense to make an honest living, and was unable to support and protect his wife. The wife too, had no wish to go with him since he was a stranger to her; under the circumstances she could neither love nor respect him. A number of orthodox people in the community who saw no reason why a wife should not follow her husband even though he be a worthless man, collected funds to enable him to sue her and her parents in the British Court of Justice. The case was examined with due ceremony and the verdict was given in the man's favor, according to Hindu law.* The wife

---

*In all cases except those directly connected with life and death, the British Government is bound according to

was doomed to go with him. Fortunately she was soon released from this sorrowful world by cholera. Whatever may be said of the epidemics that yearly assail our country, they are not unwelcome among the unfortunate women who are thus persecuted by social, religious and State laws. Many women put an end to their earthly sufferings by committing suicide. Suits at law between husband and wife are remarkable for their rarity in the British Courts in India, owing to the ever submissive conduct of women who suffer silently, knowing that the gods and justice always favor the men.

The case of Rakhmabai, that has lately profoundly agitated Hindu society, is only one of thousands of the same class. The remarkable thing about her is that she is a well-educated lady, who was brought up under the loving care of her father, and had

---

the treaties concluded with the inhabitants of India, not to interfere with their social and religious customs and laws; judicial decisions are given accordingly.

learned from him how to defend herself against the assaults of social and religious bigotries. But as soon as her father died the man who claimed to be her husband, brought suit against her in the court of Bombay. The young woman bravely defended herself, declining to go to live with the man on the ground that the marriage that was concluded without her consent could not be legally considered as such. Mr. Justice Pinhey, who tried the case in the first instance, had a sufficient sense of justice to refuse to force the lady to live with her husband against her will. Upon hearing this decision, the conservative party all over India rose as one man and girded their loins to denounce the helpless woman and her handful of friends. They encouraged the alleged husband to stand his ground firmly, threatening the British government with public displeasure if it failed to keep its agreement to force the woman to go to live with the husband according to Hindu law. Large sums were collected for the benefit of this man, Dadajee, to enable him to appeal against the decision to the full bench, whereupon, to the horror of all right-thinking people, the chief-justice sent back the case to the lower court for re-trial on its merits, as judged by the Hindu laws. The painful termination of this trial, I have in a letter written by my dear friend Rakhmabai herself, bearing date Bombay, March 18th, 1887. I quote from her letter:

"The learned and civilized judges of the full bench are determined to enforce, in this enlightened age, the inhuman laws enacted in barbaric times, four thousand years ago. They have not only commanded me to go to live with the man, but also have obliged me to pay the costs of the dispute. Just think of this extraordinary decision! Are we not living under the impartial British government, which boasts of giving equal justice to all, and are we not ruled by the Queen-Empress Victoria, herself a woman? My dear friend, I shall have been cast into the State prison when this letter reaches you; this is because I do not, and cannot obey the order of Mr. Justice Farran.

"There is no hope for women in India, whether they be under Hindu rule or British rule; some are of the opinion that my case so cruelly decided, may bring about a better condition for woman by turning public opinion in her favor, but I fear it will be otherwise. The hard-hearted mothers-in-law will now be greatly strengthened, and will induce their sons, who have for some reason or other, been slow to enforce the conjugal rights to sue their wives in the British Courts, since they are now fully assured that under no circumstances can the British government act adversely to the Hindu law."

Taught by the experience of the past, we are not at all surprised at this decision of the Bombay court. Our only wonder is that a defenseless woman like Rakhmabai dared to raise her voice in the face of the powerful Hindu law, the mighty British government, the one hundred and twenty-nine million men and the three hundred and thirty million gods of the Hindus, all these having conspired together to crush her into nothingness. We cannot blame the English government for not defending a helpless woman; it is only fulfilling its agreement made with the male population of India. How very true are the words of the Saviour, "Ye cannot serve God and Mammon." Should England serve God by protecting a helpless woman against the powers and principalities of ancient institutions, Mammon would surely be displeased, and British profit and rule in India might be endangered thereby. Let us wish it success, no matter if that success be achieved at the sacrifice of the rights and the comfort of over one hundred million women.

Meanwhile, we shall patiently await the advent of the kingdom of righteousness, wherein the weak, the lowly and the helpless shall be made happy because the great Judge Himself "shall wipe away all tears from their eyes."

CHAPTER V.

WIDOWHOOD.

WE now come to the worst and most dreaded period of a high-caste woman's life. Throughout India, widowhood is regarded as the punishment for a horrible crime or crimes committed by the woman in her former existence upon earth. The period of punishment may be greater or less, according to the nature of the crime. Disobedience and disloyalty to the husband, or murdering him in an earlier existence are the chief crimes punished in the present birth by widowhood.

If the widow be a mother of sons, she is not usually a pitiable object; although she is certainly looked upon as a sinner, yet social abuse and hatred are greatly dimished in virtue of the fact that she is a mother of the superior beings. Next in rank to her stands an ancient widow, because a virtuous, aged widow who has bravely withstood the thousand temptations and persecutions of her lot commands an involuntary respect from all people, to which may be added the honor given to old age quite independent of the individual. The widow-mother of girls is treated indifferently and sometimes with genuine hatred, especially so, when her daughters have not been given in marriage in her husband's life-time. But it is the child-widow or a childless young widow upon whom in an especial manner falls the abuse and hatred of the community as the greatest criminal upon whom Heaven's judgment has been pronounced.

In ancient times when the code of Manu was yet in the dark future and when the priesthood had not yet mutilated the original reading of a Vedic text concerning widows, a custom of re-marriage was in existence.

Widowhood.

Its history may be briefly stated :—The rite of child-marriage left many a girl a widow before she knew what marriage was, and her husband having died sonless had no right to enter into heaven and enjoy immortality, for "the father throws his debts on the son and obtains immortality if he sees the face of a living son. It is declared in the Vedas, endless are the worlds of those who have sons; there is no place for the man who is destitute of male offspring." The greatest curse that could be pronounced on enemies, was "may our enemies be destitute of offspring."

In order that these young husbands might attain the abodes of the blessed, the ancient sages invented the custom of "appointment" by which as among the Jews, the Hindu Aryans raised up seed for the deceased husband. The husband's brother, cousin or other kinsman successively was "appointed" and duly authorized to raise up offspring to the dead. The desired issue having been obtained any intercourse between the appointed persons was thenceforth considered illegal and sinful.

The woman still remained the widow of her deceased husband, and her children by the appointment were considered his heirs. Later on, this custom of "appointment" was gradually discouraged in spite of the Vedic text already quoted "there is no place for the man who is destitute of male offspring."

The duties of a widow are thus described in the code of Manu :—

> "At her pleasure let her emaciate her body by living on pure flowers, roots and fruit ; but she must never even mention the name of another man after her husband has died."
>
> "Until death let her be patient of hardships, self-controlled, and chaste, and strive to fulfil that most excellent duty which is prescribed for wives who have one husband only."—*Manu* v., 157, 158.
>
> " . . . . Nor is a second husband anywhere prescribed for virtuous women."—*Manu* v., 162.
>
> "A virtuous wife who after the death of her husband constantly remains chaste, reaches heaven, . . . "—*Manu* v., 160.
>
> "In reward of such conduct, a female who controls her thoughts, speech, and actions, gains in this life highest

Widowhood. 73

renown, and in the next world a place near her husband."*—*Manu* v., 166.

The following are the rules for a widower:—

"A twice-born man, versed in the sacred law, shall burn a wife of equal caste who conducts herself thus and dies before him, with the sacred fires used for the Agnihotra, and with the sacrificial implements."

"Having thus at the funeral, given the sacred fires to his wife who dies before him, he may marry again, and again kindle the (nuptial) fires."

" .... And having taken a wife, he must dwell in his own house during the second period of his life.—*Manu* v., 167–169.

The self-immolation of widows on their deceased husband's pyre was evidently a custom invented by the priesthood after the code of Manu was compiled. The laws taught in the schools of Apastamba, Asvalayana and others older than Manu do not mention it,

---

* It should be borne in mind that according to the popular belief there is no other heaven to a woman than the seat or mansion of her husband, where she shares the heavenly bliss with him in the next world if she be faithful to him in thought, word and deed. The only place where she can be independent of him is in hell.

neither does the code of Manu. The code of Vishnu which is comparatively recent, says, that a woman "after the death of her husband should either lead a virtuous life or ascend the funeral pile of her husband."—*Vishnu* xxv., 2.

It is very difficult to ascertain the motives of those who invented the terrible custom of the so-called Suttee, which was regarded as a sublimely meritorious act. As Manu the greatest authority next to the Vedas did not sanction this sacrifice, the priests saw the necessity of producing some text which would overcome the natural fears of the widow as well as silence the critic who should refuse to allow such a horrid rite without strong authority. So the priests said there was a text in the Rig-veda which according to their own rendering reads thus :—

"Om! let these women, not to be widowed, good wives, adorned with collyrium, holding clarified butter, consign themselves to the fire! Immortal, not childless, not husbandless, well adorned with gems, let them pass into the fire whose original element is water."

Here was an authority greater than that of Manu or of any other law giver, which could not be disobeyed. The priests and their allies, pictured heaven in the most beautiful colors and described various enjoyments so vividly that the poor widow became madly impatient to get to the blessed place in company with her departed husband. Not only was the woman assured of her getting into heaven by this sublime act, but also that by this great sacrifice she would secure salvation to herself and husband, and to their families to the seventh generation. Be they ever so sinful, they would surely attain the highest bliss in heaven, and prosperity on earth. Who would not sacrifice herself if she were sure of such a result to herself and her loved ones? Besides this, she was conscious of the miseries and degradation to which she would be subjected now that she had survived her husband. The momentary agony of suffocation in the flames was nothing compared to her lot as a widow. She gladly consented and voluntarily offered herself to please the gods and men. The rite of Suttee is thus described:—

"The widow bathed, put on new and bright garments, and, holding Kusha grass in her left hand, sipped water from her right palm, scattered some Tila grains, and then, looking eastward, quietly said, 'Om! on this day I, such and such a one, of such a family, die in the fire, that I may meet Arundhati, and reside in Svarga; that the years of my sojourn there may be as many as the hairs upon my husband, many scores multiplied; that I may enjoy with him the facilities of heaven, and bless my maternal and paternal ancestors, and those of my lord's line; that praised by Apsarasas, I may go far through the fourteen regions of Indra; that pardon may be given to my lord's sins whether he have ever killed a Brahman, broken the laws of gratitude and truth, or slain his friend. Now I do ascend this funeral pile of my husband, and I call upon you, guardians of the eight regions of the world, of sun, moon, air, of the fire, the ether, the earth and the water, and my own soul. Yama, King of Death, and you, Day, Night and Twilight, witness that I die for my beloved, by his side upon his funeral pile.' Is it wonderful that the passage of the Sati to her couch of flame was like a public festival, that the sick and sorrowful prayed her to touch them with her little, fearless, conquering hand, that criminals were let loose if she looked upon them, that the horse which carried her was never used again for earthly service?" (E. Arnold.)

The act was supposed to be altogether a

voluntary one, and no doubt it was so in many cases. Some died for the love stronger than death which they cherished for their husbands. Some died not because they had been happy in this world, but because they believed with all the heart that they should be made happy hereafter. Some to obtain great renown, for tombstones and monuments were erected to those who thus died, and afterwards the names were inscribed on the long list of family gods; others again, to escape the thousand temptations, and sins and miseries which they knew would fall to their lot as widows. Those who from pure ambition or from momentary impulse, declared their intentions thus to die, very often shrank from the fearful altar; no sooner did they feel the heat of the flames than they tried to leap down and escape the terrible fate; but it was too late. They had taken the solemn oath which must never be broken, priests and other men were at hand to force them to remount the pyre. In Bengal, where this custom was most in practice, countless, fearful tragedies of this description occurred even after British rule was long established there. Christian missionaries petitioned the government to abolish this inhuman custom, but they were told that the social and religious customs of the people constituted no part of the business of the government, and that their rule in India might be endangered by such interference. The custom went on unmolested until the first quarter of the present century, when a man from among the Hindus, Raja Ram Mohun Roy, set his face against it, and declared that it was not sanctioned by the Veda as the priests claimed. He wrote many books on this subject, showing the wickedness of the act, and with the noble co-operation of a few friends, he succeeded at last in getting the government to abolish it. Lord William Bentinck, when Governor-general of India, had the moral courage to enact the famous law of 1829, prohibiting the Suttee rite within British domains, and holding as criminals, subject to capital punishment, those who countenanced it. But it was not until 1844 that the law had any effect upon orthodox Hindu minds.

That the text quoted from the Veda was mistranslated, and a part of it forged, could have been easily shown had all Brahmans known the meaning of the Veda. The Vedic language is the oldest form of Sanskrit, and greatly differs from the later form. Many know the Vedas by heart and repeat them without a mistake, but few indeed, are those that know the meaning of the texts they repeat. "The Rig-veda," says Max Muller, "so far from enforcing the burning of widows, shows clearly that this custom was not sanctioned during the earliest period of Indian history. According to the hymns of the Rig-veda, and the Vedic ceremonial contained in the Grihya-sutras, the wife accompanies the corpse of her husband to the funeral pile, but she is there addressed with a verse taken from the Rig-veda, and ordered to leave her husband and to return to the world of the living."

"'Rise, woman,' it is said, 'come to the world of life, thou sleepest nigh unto him whose life is gone. Come to us. Thou hast thus fulfilled the duties of a wife to the husband, who once took thy hand and made thee a mother.'"

"This verse is preceded by the very verse which the later Brahmans have falsified and quoted in support of their cruel tenet. The reading of the verse is beyond all doubt, for there is no various reading, in our sense of the word, in the whole of Rig-veda. Besides, we have the commentaries and the ceremonials, and nowhere is there any difference to the text or its meaning. It is addressed to the other women who are present at the funeral, and who have to pour oil and butter on the pile .

"'May these women who are not widows, but have good husbands, draw near with oil and butter. These who are mothers may go up first to the altar, without tears. without sorrow, but decked with fine jewels.'"

It was by falsifying a single syllable that the unscrupulous priests managed to change entirely the meaning of the whole verse. Those who know the Sanskrit characters can easily understand that the falsification very likely originated in the carelessness of the transcriber or copyist, but for all that the priests who permitted the error are not excusable in the least. Instead of comparing the verse with its context, they translated it as their fancy dictated and thus under the pretext of religion they have been the cause of destroying countless lives for more than two thousand years.

Now that the Suttee-rite, partly by the will of the people and partly by the law of the empire, is prohibited, many good people feel easy in their minds, thinking that the Hindu widow has been delivered from the hand of her terrible fate; but little do they realize the true state of affairs!

Throughout India, except in the Northwestern Provinces, women are put to the severest trial imaginable after the husband's death. The manner in which they are brought up and treated from their earliest childhood compels them to be slaves to their own petty little interests, to be passionate lovers of ornaments and of self-adornment, but no sooner does the husband die than they are deprived of every gold and silver ornament, of the bright-colored garments, and of all the things they love to have about or on their persons. The cruelty of social customs does not stop here. Among the Brahmans of Deccan the heads of all widows must be shaved regularly every fortnight. Some of the lower castes, too, have adopted this custom of shaving widows' heads, and have much pride in imitating their high-caste brethren. What woman is there who does not love the wealth of soft and glossy hair with which nature has so generously decorated her head? A Hindu woman thinks it worse than death to lose her beautiful hair. Girls of fourteen and fifteen who hardly know the reason why they are so cruelly deprived of everything they like, are often seen wearing sad countenances, their eyes swollen from shedding bitter tears. They are glad to find a dark corner where they may hide their faces as if they had done something shameful and criminal. The widow must wear a single coarse garment, white, red or brown. She must eat only one meal during the twenty-four hours of a day. She must never take part in family feasts and jubilees, with others. She must not show herself to people on auspicious occasions. A man or woman thinks it unlucky to behold a widow's face before seeing any other object in the morning. A man will postpone his journey if his path happens to be crossed by a widow at the time of his departure.

A widow is called an "inauspicious" thing. The name "rand," by which she is generally known, is the same that is borne by a Nautch girl or a harlot. The relatives and neighbors of the young widow's husband are always ready to call her bad names, and to address her in abusive language at every opportunity. There is scarcely a day of her life on which she is not cursed by these people as the cause of their beloved friend's death. The mother-in-law gives vent to her grief by using such language as, when once heard, burns into a human heart. In short, the young widow's life is rendered intolerable in every possible way. There may be exceptions to this rule, but, unhappily, they are not many. In addition to all this, the young widow is always looked upon with suspicion, and closely guarded as if she were a prisoner, for fear she may at any time bring disgrace upon the family by committing some improper act. The purpose of disfiguring her by shaving her head, by not allowing her to put ornaments or bright, beautiful garments on her person, is to render her less attractive to a man's eye. Not allowing her to eat more than once a day, and compelling her to abstain from food altogether on sacred days, is a part of the discipline by which to mortify her youthful nature and desire. She is closely confined to the house, forbidden even to associate with her female friends as often as she wishes; no man except her father, brother, uncles and her aunt-cousins (who are regarded as brothers) are allowed to see or speak with her. Her life then, destitute as it is of the least literary knowledge, void of all hope, empty of every pleasure and social advantage, becomes intolerable, a curse to herself and to society at large. She has but few persons to sympathize with her. Her own parents, with whom she lives in case her husband has no relatives, or if his relatives are unable to take care of her, do, of course, sympathize with her, but custom and religious faith have a stronger hold upon them than parental love. They, too, regard their daughter with concern, lest she bring disgrace upon their family.

It is not an uncommon thing for a young widow without occupation that may satisfy mind and heart, and unable longer to endure the slights and suspicions to which she is perpetually subjected, to escape from her prison-home. But when she gets away from it, where shall she go? No respectable family, even of a lower caste, will have her for a servant. She is completely ignorant of any art by which she may make an honest living. She has nothing but the single garment which she wears on her person. Starvation and death stare her in the face; no ray of hope penetrates her densely-darkened mind. What can she do? The only alternative before her is either to commit suicide or, worse still, accept a life of infamy and shame. Oh, cruel, cruel is the custom that drives thousands of young widows to such a fate. Here is a prayer by a woman doomed to life-long misery, which will describe her own and her sisters' feelings better than any words of mine. It was written by a pupil of a British Zenana missionary, one of the few Hindu women who can read and write, and one who has tasted the bitter sorrows and degradation of Hindu widowhood from her childhood,—

"Oh Lord, hear my prayer! No one has turned an eye on the oppression that we poor women suffer, though with weeping, and crying and desire, we have turned to all sides, hoping that some one would save us. No one has lifted up his eyelids to look upon us, nor inquire into our case. We have searched above and below, but Thou art the only One who wilt hear our complaint,—Thou knowest our impotence, our degradation, our dishonor.

"O Lord, inquire into our case. For ages dark ignorance has brooded over our minds and spirits; like a cloud of dust it rises and wraps us round, and we are like prisoners in an old and mouldering house, choked and buried in the dust of custom, and we have no strength to go out. Bruised and beaten, we are like the dry husks of the sugar-cane when the sweet juice has been extracted. All-knowing God, hear our prayer! forgive our sins and give us power of escape, that we may see something of Thy world. O Father, when shall we be set free from this jail? For what sin have we been born to live in this prison? From Thy throne of judgment justice flows, but it does not reach us; in this, our life-long misery, only injustice comes near us.

"Thou hearer of prayer, if we have sinned against Thee, forgive, but we are too ignorant to know what sin is. Must the punishment of sin fall on those who are too ignorant to know what it is? O great Lord, our name is written with drunkards, with lunatics, with imbeciles, with the very animals; as they are not responsible, we are not. Criminals, confined in the jails for life, are happier than we, for they know something of Thy world. They were not born in prison, but we have not for one day, no, not even in our dreams, seen Thy world; to us it is nothing but a name; and not having seen the world, we cannot know Thee, its maker. Those who have seen Thy works may learn to understand Thee, but for us, who are shut in, it is not possible to learn to know Thee. We see only the four walls of the house. Shall we call them the world, or India? We have been born in this jail, we have died here, and are dying.

"O Father of the world, hast Thou not created us? Or has perchance, some other god made us? Dost Thou care only for men? Hast Thou no thought for us women? Why hast Thou created us male and female? O Almighty, hast Thou not power to make us other than we are, that we too might have some share in the comforts of this life? The cry of the oppressed is heard even in the world. Then canst Thou look upon our victim hosts, and shut Thy doors of justice? O God Almighty and Unapproachable, think upon Thy mercy, which is a vast sea, and remember us. O Lord, save us, for we cannot bear our hard lot; many of us have killed ourselves, and we are still killing ourselves. O God of mercy, our prayer to Thee is this, that the curse may be removed from the women of India. Create in the hearts of the men some sympathy, that our lives may no longer be passed in vain longing, that saved by Thy mercy, we may taste something of the joys of life."

A Hindu gentleman contributes an article entitled "The Hindu Widow," to *The Nineteenth Century*. I quote from this as testimony from the other sex, of the truthfulness of my statement, lest I should appear to exaggerate the miserable condition to which my sister-widows are doomed for life :—

"The widow who has no parents has to pass her whole life under the roof of her father-in-law, and then she knows no comfort whatever. She has to meet from her late husband's relations only unkind looks and unjust reproaches. She has to work like a slave, and for the reward of all her drudgery she only receives hatred and abhorrence from her mother-in-law and sisters-in-law. If there is any disorder in the domestic arrangements of the family the widow is blamed and cursed for it. Among Hindus, women cannot inherit any paternal property, and if a widow is left any property by her husband she cannot call it her own. All her wealth belongs to her son, if she has any, and if she has nobody to inherit it she is made to adopt an heir, and give him all her property directly he comes of age, and herself live on a bare allowance granted by him. Even death cannot save a widow from indignities. For when a wife dies she is burnt in the clothes she had on, but a widow's corpse is covered with a coarse white cloth, and there is little ceremony at her funeral. . . . . .

"'The English have abolished Sati (Suttee), but alas! neither the English nor the angels know what goes on in our houses, and the Hindus not only do not care, but think it good!' Such were the words of a widow; and well might she exclaim that 'neither the English nor the angels know, and that the Hindus not only don't care, but think it good;' for Hindu as I am, I can vouch for her statement that very few Hindus have a fair knowledge of the actual sufferings of the widows among them, and fewer still care to know the evils and horrors of the barbarous custom which victimizes their own sisters and daughters in so ruthless a manner; nay, on the contrary, the majority of the orthodox Hindus consider the practice to be good and salutary. Only the Hindu widows know their own sufferings; it is perfectly impossible for any other mortal, or even 'the angels,' (as the widow says), to realize them. One can easily imagine how hard the widow's lot must be . . . . when to the continuous course of fastings, self-inflictions and humiliations is added the galling ill-treatment which she receives from her own relations and friends. To a Hindu widow death is a thousand times more welcome than her miserable existence. It is no doubt this feeling that drove in former times many widows to immolate themselves on the funeral pyres of their dead husbands."—DEVENDRA N. DAS, *Nineteenth Century, September*, 1886.

There is a class of reformers who think that they will meet all the wants of widows by establishing the re-marriage system. This system should certainly be introduced for the benefit of the infant widows who wish to marry on coming to age; but at the same time it should be remembered that this alone is incapable and insufficient to meet their wants.

In the first place, widow-marriage among the high-caste people will not for a long time become an approved custom. The old idea is too deeply rooted in the heart of society to be soon removed. Secondly, there are not many men who will boldly come forward and marry widows, even if the widows wish it. It is one thing to talk about doing things contrary to the approved custom, but to practice is quite another matter. It is now about fifty years since the movement called widow-marriage among the high-caste Hindus was started, but those who have practiced it are but few. I have known men of great learning and high reputation who took oaths to the effect that if they were to become widowers and wished to marry again they would marry widows. But no sooner had their first wives died than they forgot all about the oaths and married pretty little maidens. Society threatens them with excommunication, their friends and relatives entreat them with tears in their eyes, others offer money and maids if they will consent to give up the idea of marrying a widow. Can flesh and blood resist these temptations? If some men wish to be true to their convictions, they must be prepared to suffer perpetual martyrdom. After marrying a widow they are sure to be cut off from all connection with society and friends, and even with their nearest relatives. In such a case no faithful Hindu would ever give them assistance if they were to fall in distress or become unable to earn their daily bread; they will be ridiculed by, and hated of all men. How many people are there in the world who would make this tremendous sacrifice on the altar of conscience? The persecution to be endured by people who transgress established customs is so great that life becomes a burden. A few years ago a high-caste man in Cutch, (Northwestern India,) ventured to marry a widow, but to endure the persecution which ensued, was beyond his

Widowhood. 93

power, and the wretched fellow was soon after found dead, having committed suicide.

Re-marriage, therefore, is not available, nor would it be at all times desirable, as a mitigation of the sufferer's lot. So the poor, helpless high-caste widow with the one chance of ending her miseries in the Suttee rite taken away from her, remains as in ages past with none to help her.

CHAPTER VI.

HOW THE CONDITION OF WOMEN TELLS UPON SOCIETY.

THOSE who have done their best to keep women in a state of complete dependence and ignorance, vehemently deny that this has anything to do with the present degradation of the Hindu nation. I pass over the hundreds of nonsenses which are brought forward as the strongest reasons for keeping women in ignorance and dependence. They have already been forced out into the broad day-light of a generous civilization, and have been put to the fiery proof of science and found wanting. Above all, the noble example of thousands of women in many countries have burned the so-called reasons to ashes. But their ghosts are still hovering over the land of the Hindus and are frightening the timid and the ignorant to death. Let us hope that in God's good time, all these devils shall be forever cast out of India's body; meanwhile it is our duty to take the matter into serious consideration, and to put forth our best endeavors to hasten the glad day for India's daughters, aye, and for her sons also; because in spite of the proud assertions of our brethren that they have not suffered from the degradation of women, their own condition betrays but too plainly the contrary.

Since men and women are indissolubly united by Providence as members of the same body of human society, each must suffer when their fellow-members suffer, whether they will confess it or not. In the animal as well as in the vegetable kingdom, nature demands that all living beings shall freely comply with its conditions of growth or they cannot become that which they were originally designed to be. Why should any exception to this law be made for the purdah women? Closely confined to the four walls of their house, deprived throughout their lives of the opportunity to breathe healthy fresh air, or to drink in the wholesome sunshine, they become weaker and weaker from generation to generation, their physical statures dwarfed, their spirits crushed under the weight of social prejudices and superstitions, and their minds starved from absolute lack of literary food and of opportunity to observe the world. Thus fettered, in ninety cases out of a hundred, at the least calculation, they grow to be selfish slaves to their petty individual interests, indifferent to the welfare of their own immediate neighbors, much more to their nation's well-being. How could these imprisoned mothers be expected to bring forth children better than themselves, for as the tree and soil are, so shall the fruit be. Consequently we see all around us in India a generation of men least deserving that exalted appellation.

The doctrine of "pre-natal influence" can nowhere be more satisfactorily proved than in India. The mother's spirits being depressed, and mind as well as body weakened by the monotony and inactivity of her life, the unborn child cannot escape the evil consequences. The men of Hindustan do not when babes, suck from the mother's breast, true patriotism, and in their boyhood, the mother, poor woman, is unable to develope that divine faculty in them owing to her utter ignorance of the past and present condition of her native land. Fault-finding with neighbors, bitter feelings towards tyrant relatives expressed in words and actions, selfish interest in personal and family affairs, these are the chief lessons that children learn at the mother's knee, from babyhood up to the seventh or eighth year of age.

Again, how does it come to pass that each succeeding generation grows weaker than the one preceding it, if not because the progenitors of each generation lack the mental and physical strength which children are destined to inherit? The father may have been free and healthy in mind, as well as in body, but the mother was not; she undoubtedly has bequeathed the fatal legacy of weakness and dullness to her children. The complete submission of women under the Hindu law has in the lapse of milleniums of years converted them into slavery-loving creatures. They are glad to lean upon any one and be altogether dependent, and thus it has come to pass that their sons as a race, desire to depend upon some other nation, and not upon themselves. The seclusion, complete dependence and the absolute ignorance forced upon the mothers of our nation have been gradually and fatally telling upon the mental and physical health of the men, and in these last times they have borne the poisonous fruit that will compel the Hindu nation to die a miserable and prolonged death if a timely remedy is not taken to them.

Moreover the Hindu woman's ignorance

prevents liberal-minded and progressive men from making necessary and important changes in the manners and habits of the household; bigoted women also prevent their husbands and sons from such important enterprises as crossing the ocean in the pursuit of useful knowledge, or for purposes of trade.

To add to all the disabilities of the Hindu mother in the discharge of her sacred maternal duties, she is as a rule, wholly ignorant of the commonest hygienic laws. It must be remembered that she is herself a girl scarcely out of her babyhood, when she becomes a mother. At about fourteen, fifteen or sixteen years of age she cannot be expected to know all that is necessary in order to take good care of her child. The first and second of the children of this young mother usually die, and if they survive, they are apt to grow up to be weak and unhealthy adults. Until they are seven or eight years of age, the children of the household are left to themselves without any one to take care of them, and no influence is exerted to mould their character at this most interesting and important period of life. Who but an intelligent and loving mother can do this all-important work for her children at that age?

Having thus far endeavored to bring to the notice of Western women the condition of a class of their oriental sisters, I now desire to direct their attention definitely to our chief needs. After many years of careful observation and thought, I have come to the conclusion that the chief needs of high-caste Hindu women are :—1st, Self-Reliance ; 2nd, Education ; 3rd, Native Women Teachers.

I. Self-Reliance.—The state of complete dependence in which men are required by the law-giver to keep women from birth to the end of their lives makes it impossible for them to have self-reliance, without which a human being becomes a pitiful parasite. Women of the working classes are better off than their sisters of high castes in India, for in many cases they are obliged to depend upon themselves, and an opportunity for cultivating self-reliance is thus afforded them by which they largely profit. But high-caste women, unless their families are actually destitute of means to keep them, are shut up within the four walls of their house. In after-time, if they are left without a protector, *i. e.* a male relative to support and care for them, they literally do not know what to do with themselves. They have been so cruelly cropped in their early days that self-reliance and energy are dead within them; helpless victims of indolence and false timidity they are easily frightened out of their wits and have little or no strength to withstand the trials and difficulties which must be encountered by a person on her way toward progress. But it is idle to hope that the condition of my countrywomen will ever improve without individual self-reliance; therefore, is it not the duty of our Western sisters to teach them how they may become self-reliant?

II. Education.—The lack of education among the women of India can be fairly realized by scanning the report of the Educational Commission for 1883, and the census returns of 1880–81. Of the ninety-nine million seven hundred thousand women and girls directly under British rule, ninety-nine and one-half millions are returned as unable to read and write; the remaining two hundred thousand who are able either to read or write, cannot all be reckoned as educated, for the school-going period of a girl is generally between seven and nine years of age; within that short time she acquires little more than ability to read the second or the third vernacular reading-book, and a little knowledge of arithmetic which usually comprehends no more than the four simple rules. It should be remembered that the two hundred thousand women able to read or write are the "*alumnæ*" of the government schools, mission schools, private schools conducted by the inhabitants of India independently, private societies and Zenana mission agencies all reckoned together. It is surprising how even this small number of women can have acquired the limited knowledge indicated, when we consider the powers and principalities that are incessantly fighting against female education in India. Girls of nine and ten when recently out of school and given in marriage are wholly cut off from reading or writing, because it is a shame for a young woman or girl to hold a paper or book in her hand, or to read in the presence of others in her husband's house. It is a popular belief among high-caste women that their husbands will die if they should read or should hold a pen in their fingers. The fear of becoming a widow overcomes their hunger and thirst for knowledge. Moreover the little wives can get but scanty time to devote to self-culture; any one fortunate enough to possess the desire and able to command the time is in constant fear of being seen by her husband's relatives. Her employment cannot long be kept secret where every one is on the lookout, and when discovered she is ridiculed, laughed at and even commanded by the elders to leave off this nonsense. Her literary pursuits are now at an end unless the proceedings of the elders be interfered with by her progressive husband; but alas, such husbands are extremely rare. Our schools, too, are not very attractive to children; the teachers of primary schools, (and it is to these schools that girls are usually sent), are but nominally educated, and do not know how to make the lessons interesting for children. Consequently a great many of the girls who have been educated up to the second or third standard (grade) in these primary schools make it their business quickly to forget their lessons as soon as they find an opportunity. Shut in from the world and destitute of the ability to engage in newspaper and useful book-reading, they have little or no knowledge of common things around them, and of the most important events that are daily occurring in their own or foreign lands.

Ignorant, unpatriotic, selfish and uncultivated, they drag the men down with them into the dark abyss where they dwell together without hope, without ambition to be something or to do something in the world.

III. Native Women Teachers.—American and English women as Zenana missionaries are doing all they can to elevate and enlighten India's daughters. These good people deserve respect and praise from all, and the heart-felt thanks of those for whose elevation they toil, but the disabilities of an unfriendly climate, and of an unknown tongue make it exceedingly difficult for them to enter upon their work for some time after reaching India; and then, "what are these among so many?" They are literally lost among the nearly one hundred millions of women under British rule to whom must be added several millions more under Hindu and Mahommedan rule. In America and in England we hear encouraging reports from mission fields, which state that a few thousand Hindu and Mahommedan women and girls are being instructed in schools or in their own homes, but these seem as nothing, compared to the vast multitude of the female population of Hindustan. In a country where castes and the seclusion of women are regarded as essential tenets of the national creed, we can scarcely hope for a general spread of useful knowledge among women, through either men of their own race or through foreign women. All experience in the past history of mankind has shown that efforts for the elevation of a nation must come from within and work outward to be effectual.

The one thing needful, therefore, for the general diffusion of education among women in India is a body of persons from among themselves who shall make it their life-work to teach by precept and example their fellow-countrywomen.

CHAPTER VII.

THE APPEAL.

IN the preceding chapters I have tried to tell my readers briefly the sad story of my countrywomen, and also to bring to their notice what are our chief needs. We, the women of India, are hungering and thirsting for knowledge; only education under God's grace, can give us the needful strength to rise up from our degraded condition.

Our most pressing want and one which must immediately be met is women-teachers of our own nationality. How can these women-teachers be supplied? I have long been thinking over this matter and now I am prepared to give answer.

Among the inhabitants of India, the high-caste people rank as the most intelligent; they have been a refined and cultivated race for more than two thousand years. The women of these castes have been and still are kept in ignorance, yet they have inherited from their fathers to a certain degree, quickness of perception and intelligence. A little care and judicious education bestowed upon them will make many of them competent teachers and able workers. That this statement is not altogether visionary on my part, has been proven by the gratifying results of careful training in the person of Chandramukhi Bose, M. A., now lady principal of Bethune School, Calcutta, Kadambini B. Ganguli, B. A., M. B., and also others who have successfully passed their examinations in the Calcutta University. The professors of the Woman's Medical College of Pennsylvania will bear testimony to the ability of the late Dr. Anandibai Joshee. Had her life been spared a little longer she would have shown to the world that the Hindu woman, in spite of all drawbacks equals any woman of civilized countries.

Again, according to the census of 1881 there were in India twenty million nine hundred and thirty thousand six hundred and twenty-six widows, of all ages and castes. Among these were six hundred and sixty-nine thousand one hundred widows under nineteen years of age, viz.:

Under nine years of age 78,976
From 10 to 14 years of age. . . . 207,388
From 15 to 19 years of age. . . . 382,736
                                                           669,100

Girls of nine and ten, or thirteen years of age, whose betrothed husbands are dead, are virgin widows, and these, if of high-caste families, must remain single throughout life. Now if there were suitable educational institutions where young widows who might wish to be independent of their relatives and make an honest living for themselves, might go to be instructed in useful handiwork, and educated for teachers, many horrid occurrences might be prevented, and at the same time these widows would prove a welcome blessing to their countrywomen. But alas! institutions have not been founded anywhere in India where high-caste widows can receive shelter and education.

In the year 1866, an eminent English lady, Miss Mary Carpenter, made a short tour in India, with a view to find some way by which women's condition in that country might be improved. She at once discovered that the chief means by which the desired end might be accomplished was by furnishing women-teachers for the Hindu zenanas. She suggested that the British government should establish normal schools for training women-teachers and that scholarships should be awarded to girls in order to prolong their school-going period, and to assist indigent women, who would otherwise be unable to pursue their studies. In response to Miss Carpenter's appeal upon her return to England, the British government founded several schools for women in

India, and in honor of this good lady a few "Mary Carpenter scholarships" were endowed by benevolent persons. These schools which I have personally inspected, were opened to women of every caste, and while they have undoubtedly been of use, they have not realized the hopes of their founder, partly because of the impossibility of keeping caste-rules in them, and partly on account of the inadequacy of the arrangements for attendance. When a high-caste widow takes it upon herself to go to school, she cannot hope, except in cases which are extremely rare, to receive any kind of help from her own relatives; so she is thrown out a penniless, helpless, forlorn creature to face the world alone. If then she is so fortunate as to be sheltered in a normal school and is awarded a studentship she finds this scarcely enough to keep her from starvation, its money value being from twelve to twenty or twenty-five dollars per year; but she cannot get even this scanty support from the educational department, unless she pass a certain examination. How can an illiterate widow hope to pass that examination?

Besides these government normal schools for women, of which at the present time, there are probably six throughout all India, there are a few foreign mission schools where a woman may find shelter and instruction, but if she be an orthodox Hindu by faith, and of a respectable family, she will on no account take refuge with people of a strange religion and country. There are exceptions of course to this statement, but as a rule, a high-caste Hindu woman prefers death to this alternative. She knows that if she goes to live with missionaries she must lose caste, and that she must study their Bible, and perhaps in the end be induced to forsake her ancestral faith and embrace a strange one. No woman of any religion in which she firmly believes whether it appear to others to be true or false, would violate her conscience simply for food and shelter. That the fear of being tempted to abjure one's religion for the sake of worldly gain should prevent many an excellent Hindu widow from going to foreign missionary schools is undoubted. She honestly believes that if her life is rendered intolerable by domestic misery she can drown herself in some sacred river by which deed she will not only escape the wretchedness of this life, but her past sins will be forgiven, and a place in heaven secured, but to forsake her ancestral religion under any circumstances would doom her to eternal perdition in the world to come.

Is there then no way of helping and educating these high-caste widows? Can none of these obstacles be removed from her path? Yes! they can be removed, and the course which in my judgment can most advantageously be taken in order to succor the widows and the women of India in general, may be stated as follows :—

I. Houses should be opened for the young and high-caste child-widows where they can take shelter without the fear of losing their caste, or of being disturbed in their religious belief and where they may have entire freedom of action as relates to caste-rules, such as cooking of food, etc., provided they do not violate the rules or disturb the peace of the house wherein they have taken up their abode.

II. In order to help them make an honorable and independent living, they should be taught in these houses to be teachers, governesses, nurses and housekeepers, and should become skilled in other forms of hand-work, according to their taste and capacity.

III. These houses should be under the superintendence and management of influential Hindu ladies and gentlemen, who should be pledged to make each house a happy home and an instructive institution for those who seek its opportunities.

IV. The services of well-qualified American ladies as assistants and teachers should be secured in order to afford the occupants of the houses the combined advantage of Eastern and Western civilization and education.

V. Libraries containing the best books on

history, science, art, religions and other departments of literature should be established in these houses for the benefit of their inmates and of other women in their vicinity who may wish to read. Lectureships should also be established in the libraries, and the lecturers should be engaged with the distinct understanding that they do not speak irreverently of any religion or sacred custom while lecturing in that house or library; the lecturers should embrace in their topics, hygiene, geography, elementary science, foreign travel, etc., and the lectures should be designed primarily to open the eyes and ears of those who long have dwelt in the prison-house of ignorance, knowing literally nothing of God's beautiful world.

It is my intention after my return home (which I trust may be within a year from this time) to establish at least one such institution. I am fully aware of the great responsibility the trial—and it may be the failure—will involve; but as some one must make a beginning, I am resolved to try, trusting that God, who knows the need of my country-women, will raise up able workers to forward this cause, whether I succeed in it or not. The great majority of my country-people being most bitterly opposed to the education of women, there is little hope of my getting from them either good words or pecuniary aid.

For the present it is useless to reason with high-caste Hindu gentlemen concerning this matter; they only ridicule the proposal or silently ignore it. There are some among them who would certainly approve and would help to carry the idea into effect, but they must first realize its advantages and see its good results. One must have the power of performing miracles to induce this class of men to receive the gospel of society's well-being through the elevation of woman. Such a miracle I have faith to believe will be performed in India before the end of the next ten years, and if this be true, the enterprise will prove self-supporting after that period with only native aid. There is even now a handful of Hindus entertaining progressive ideas who are doing all they can to reform the religious and social customs of Hindustan, and who will, without doubt, support my work from the beginning; but they have little with which to forward the cause except their personal services.

An institution of the kind indicated, where the pupils must be supported and the foreign teachers liberally paid for their services, cannot be founded and afterwards kept in a flourishing condition without money. Therefore I invite all good women and men of the United States to give me their help liberally in whatever way they may be able for a period of about ten years; it is my solemn belief that it is the most sacred duty of those who dwell in this highly-favored land to bestow freely talents of whatever kind they may possess to help forward this educational movement. I venture to make this appeal because I believe that those who regard the preaching of the gospel of our Lord Jesus Christ to the heathen so important as to spend in its accomplishment millions of money and hundreds of valuable lives will deem it of the first importance to prepare the way for the spread of the gospel by throwing open the locked doors of the Indian zenanas, which cannot be done safely without giving suitable education to the women, whereby they will be able to bear the dazzling light of the outer world and the perilous blasts of social persecution.

Mothers and fathers, compare the condition of your own sweet darlings at your happy firesides with that of millions of little girls of a corresponding age in India, who have already been sacrificed on the unholy altar of an inhuman social custom, and then ask yourselves whether you can stop short of doing something to rescue the little widows from the hands of their tormentors. Millions of heart-rending cries are daily rising from within the stony walls of Indian zenanas; thousands of child-widows are annually dying without a ray of hope to cheer their hearts, and other thousands are daily being crushed under a fearful weight of sin and shame, with no one to prevent their ruin by providing for them a better way.

Will you not, all of you who read this book, think of these, my countrywomen, and rise, moved by a common impulse, to free them from life-long slavery and infernal misery? I beg you, friends and benefactors, educators and philanthropists, all who have any interest in or compassion for your fellow-creatures, let the cry of India's daughters, feeble though it be, reach your ears and stir your hearts. In the name of humanity, in the name of your sacred responsibilities as workers in the cause of humanity, and, above all, in the most holy name of God, I summon you, true women and men of America, to bestow your help quickly, regardless of nation, caste or creed.

www.ingramcontent.com/pod-product-compliance
Lightning Source LLC
Chambersburg PA
CBHW030435190426
43202CB00036B/1128